The Moon She Rocks You

Revealing the Secrets of Women's Inner Emotions

Gurutej Khalsa

The Moon She Rocks You

Note to the Reader

This book contains useful information, however, the author and publisher do not hold any liability.

This information in this book is for educational and informational purposes only. Always seek the advice of someone qualified in this field for any questions you may have.

Contents

Dedication

"To the women of the world, that you may experience both your power and your grace."

—*Gurutej Khalsa*

Testimonials

"Gurutej is a true gift to the yoga world. She is able to communicate the living ancient wisdom of Kundalini yoga through her natural and practical teaching on the Moon Centers which vibrates with flowing consciousness. Gurutej awakens through her love of sharing the secrets of women from within and her teachings in her book which will resonate with women and men at all levels of experience on the spiritual path."

—*Lisa Scanandolri, co-founder of Lisa's Yoga*

"Had I known how revealing this was and what great solutions for my problems, I would have willingly paid you almost anything."

—*J. Toronto*

"I studied the Moon Centers in Yogi Bhajan's class. Gurutej explains them in such depth, it is astounding. She makes them easy, accessible, and fun. This is not just for women. My husband has been taking an interest in this and that has made life so much better. You need this. Don't wait."

—*Siri Bandhu, preventative medicine business planner*

"What an amazing program! I am still learning more every day. That is what I call a good deal; the program that keeps giving me more."

—*Pat A., L.A*

About the Author

To know Gurutej Khalsa, you first need to know her name, which means "the one who brings you from darkness into light at the speed of light." What she teaches emanates from her name and her purpose to lead others towards their inner self by mastering their own energy.

Even at six years old, she already had the vocation to help others connect to their essence through healing, meditation, yoga, and chanting. She is a born leader, a creational genius, and a true inspirational visionary. Her boundless energy enlivens the day and her gift for lightness, comedy, and humor radiates with every breath and every word of her powerful message. Gurutej is one of Yogi Bhajan's original disciples and close collaborators. She is a true Master Teacher of Kundalini Yoga.

With over 40 years of yoga experience, Gurutej has created products that teach mastery of personal energy to enrich people's lives. She is the creator of: 4 yoga videos (two of which are among the top 10 yoga DVDs of all time), aromatherapy Chakra Pillows, the book, A Slice of the Beloved, and a series of ingenious video workshops, including Get Your Skinny Back.

This new book reveals the meaning, gifts, effects, and challenges of the Moon Centers of the female body and how they allow a deeper understanding of their quirks and nuances. It explains why we should pay attention to these Moon Centers and know how to live a better life through them.

Gurutej has established yoga centers throughout the United States and Canada. They all reflect her enduring dedication to alternative education, children, the homeless, community outreach, philanthropy, and conscious living. Her efforts have always been and still are, tireless.

For more information about:

A Slice of the Beloved –

http://gurutej.com/store/books-of-enlightenment/yoga-for-couples/

Get Your Skinny Back –

http://gurutej.com/hww-skinny-back-download

About the Book

Have you noticed that some days you feel strong and powerful and can take on the entire universe and other days you want to find a bathroom to hide in and cry? Why is that? This book will give you many tools, techniques and tips to restore your balance so you can easily access the gifts of each Moon Center. This is not a shield to hide behind, but information to make you more aware, informed, and complete with support tools that will make you more powerful as a woman.

Women are ruled by the moon. Like the moon, women are a mystery. We have a dark unseen side and another that's fully lit. We change cycles every 2.5 days. We have tides like the ocean, and we call our menstrual cycle, our moon cycle. The Moon Centers show us various points in our body that correspond to certain feelings and moods we may experience during the 28-day lunar cycle.

The cycle of the moon plays with these points of your body. What I would like to accomplish in this book is to explain these points; show where they reside in a woman's body and reveal what the locations mean for each of these Moon Centers. But this book is not only about knowing what and where the Moon Centers are in your body, it's also about revealing how their cycles can be used to your advantage. This book will give you a preview of some tools and tips you can utilize to help balance these Centers and to activate them.

With The Moon She Rocks You, you can use a chart of the body and check it each day to see where you think you are in the cycle. You will also get in depth information on the negative, positive, and neutral aspects of each Moon Center and how these play out with ways for balancing each of them. With practice, you can make great use of the Moon Centers in your life.

(http://gurutej.com/store/11-moon-centers)

Introduction

You're a woman…
1. Do you want to be calm and centered?
2. Do you feel you could be less reactive, judgmental, and stressed?
3. Do you wish you could be on top of your emotions?

Let's face it, many women have out-of-control emotions—huge emotional swings that they often blame on PMS, SMS, MPS—whatever! Some people would say it's easier to just let the emotions rule. Wrong. As a woman, I'm sure that you'd welcome knowing that there are ways other than prescription drugs, to deal with your emotions—how to get them to work for you instead of the other way around—being a slave to them. Because you've taken the time to open this book and read it, I'm sure you agree.

I took the time to write this book and share it with all women out there because you can easily learn about the Moon Centers and unearth the gifts inside each of them. It wasn't as easy as picking up a book for me. I learned about them at a women's camp, I don't remember exactly which one. Yogi Bhajan spoke about the Moon Centers for about half an hour. We found it interesting at the time, but that was all.

Some ten years later, while sorting out my notes, I found this amazing material again and decided to study it, try it, and share it. If you are a woman, knowing about The Moon Centers gives you power over your negative emotions. If you are a man, it gives you the key to understand women of all ages. You learn to listen to the voice of their emotions.

For instance, if your energy is in the Clitoris point and it is in a challenged state, it's not advisable to go on a first date. Why? Because this makes you want to be with people you know well, who make you feel comfortable. You want to be with your girl friends and do things that are comforting to you and them. If you go on a blind date then, you won't feel interest for the other person. You will sit there wishing to be at home curled up on the sofa watching your favorite movie for the tenth time or at Nina's pajamas party.

The Moon Centers gave me the power of choice. Knowing which Center my energy was in and in which of the three states I was in (positive, neutral, or challenged), saved me from a lot of drama and trauma, as I like to say. I knew why I felt this or that way, and I knew how to make the most of it. I didn't need to change or hide the emotions, once I understood them. It was exhilarating! I wasn't crazy.

Knowing about the Moon Centers definitely helps any person who is hurting from something, like a painful divorce or separation. It certainly helped me when I was going through my marriage troubles.

Men can also benefit from having this knowledge. I am convinced that all women want three things from men. First: They want to be heard and really listened to, so they don't have to keep repeating things. Second: They want to be seen, which is why they ask you how they look in this dress or that new hairdo. Third: They want to be respected, unconditionally, when they are great or when they are not.

The Moon She Rocks You

By applying the easy techniques shown here, men can learn how to properly support their special woman and all the women in their life. My wish is that women—you—make the most of this knowledge and feel supported in being the best and most expansive you.

What are the gifts of the Moon Centers and how do you use these to improve your life? I invite you to come see for yourself.

—Gurutej

Challenges Encountered by Women

What's the Problem with Women?

What makes them so unpredictable at times? What makes them confusing to men and at the same time be awesome and worthy of their attention? What makes women so intriguing? What makes them behave the way they do?

The pull of the moon creates tides in women. It pulls on your bodily fluids just as it pulls on the oceans and creates the cycles of the tides. The moon, which rules women, is about mystery, magic, and emotions. This makes women emotional, unpredictable, and mind blowing!

Women change cycles every 2.5 days. So I always say if you don't like the way your woman is behaving today, come back after 2.5 days and they will be entirely different—such awesome unpredictability! Here we will shed light on the mystery and unpredictability in women and how she can become more calm, creative and empowered.

How Can the Moon Centers Help Women?

During your emotional outbursts, how many hours in a week do you have spend doing damage control? How much money would you spend just to ease the frustration and tension within you? What do you do to cope? You realize that many solutions are merely superficial means for you to get out of the emotional turmoil you are experiencing. The Moon Centers, however, would give you the capacity to access your gifts and not be drugged by your emotions.

If you work on your Moon Centers through meditation, exercise, and by learning to listen to your intuition, your life as a woman will become less stressful. You will learn to live in harmony with yourself and with others. You will be endowed with grace, happiness, and power. No other external solution can give women any of these gifts.

Discovering the Gifts inside Women's Emotions

How do women get their emotions to work for them instead of them working for their emotions or being their slave? The Moon Centers reveal the answer to these queries.

With the complete The Moon She Rocks You program, you can learn to chart your cycle and check each day to see where you are in this cycle. Once you have plotted your particular cycle—and this often takes a few months of paying attention—it will stay the same unless you undergo some huge trauma or shift in your life. I suggest you get a few friends to do this with you. It will not only make the activity more fun, but will also help you achieve a less biased awareness as you help each other figure out which cycle you are in.

Remember, it will take a few months before you will really have your cycle plotted. This requires that you tune in with your emotional states, which can be either subtle or obvious. If you are able to do this properly, you are assured of tranquility and comfort.

19

The Moon She Rocks You

You will know who you are and the gifts that are asleep within you.

Imagine how your life would be, if during challenging days, you could clear your head just by working on your Moon Centers. Remember, grace is your birthright, power is your gift, and happiness is your cloak. Once you are familiar with all of the Centers, plot them out and work with them. It would be happiness and power rolled into one. It's a priceless blessing!

So, are you ready to be aware and enlightened? Let's start with the description of the Moon Centers.

The 11 Moon Centers of a Woman

Location	Positive	Challenged	Neutral
Hairline	Visionary	Paranoid	Nothing can move you
Eyebrows	Healing Dreams	Fantasy Illusions	Using Visions
Cheeks	Promotion Queen	Out of control flirting	Radiant/ beautiful
Lips	Talkative	Sharp Tongued	Excellent communication for higher goals
Earlobes	Discussions of life	Self-Deprecating	Empowered by values
Nape of Neck	Romantic voice	Unable to communicate	Speaking from heart
Nipples	Compassionate over giving	Victim	Neutral unconditional love
Belly Button	Physical Energy	Unstable	Power to show up
Inner Thighs	Highly Organized	Disorganized	Creative Strength
Clitoris	Needs to socialize	Clannish/ Cliquish	Leadership/ Charming
Membranes of the Vagina	Energetic/ Connective	Empty/Zero	Beginnings and endings all the same

What Moon Center You Are In?

These are the items you will need for this exercise which will assist you in correctly locating your moon center: paper, a pen, and a pendulum, which can all be purchased online or from alternative book stores, some health food stores, and any store that sells crystals.

- Take a blank sheet of paper, like the ones you use for your home printer.

- Fold it longitudinally to have a slim rectangle.

- At the top of it, write a big YES; at the bottom of it write a big NO.

- Now breathe very deeply and relax, thinking of the Moon Centers. Have the list of those nearby. Take your pendulum and start asking: Am I in the Hairline Center right now? The pendulum will oscillate and go to the answer. Keep on asking about each center until it stops over the YES.

- If you don't have a pendulum, you can create one with a gold chain and ring.

Make sure you don't feel any pain or even the slightest discomfort holding the pendulum, otherwise it won't work. You can easily find photos and videos on how to hold it properly on the Internet. Isn't that easy?

We are going to discuss each Center and I will give you techniques that you can do to get yourself out of the challenged and into neutral or positive aspect of each one. Remember these are gifts, and it's really up to you how you use them. Each Center has a gift (the positive aspect) and a distraction (the challenged aspect) which takes away from the attraction (the neutral aspect) which is the vastest space to live out of.

Hairline

Overview

When the moon is in the Hairline, you will feel very visionary if you are balanced. If you are challenged, you will feel paranoid and afraid. With both the positive and the challenged aspects, the mantra for this position is, "Nothing can move you." You are fixed in your vision and you *know* what you know. You are not easily swayed and this goes for both the balanced and challenged states. You can be very fixed in your fear and insecurity if you are challenged. Balanced, you are like a luminary that everyone looks up to.

The Details

What is the Hairline Center about? The interesting thing is that a lot of societies in history have thought certain hairlines are really beautiful and others are not. There was a time when people actually plucked their hair so that they could have a hairline that follows cultural norms. Oh, my God! Can you imagine how that practice messed with this Moon Center?

24

But what's the Hairline Moon Center, anyway? It's about vision! The Hairline is a beautiful place of vision and it's about you being a visionary. When you are a visionary, you allow the moon to reveal the mysteries of all infinity to you and through you. But sometimes, a person can get really scared of that. It's because in many parts of the world, it's not safe to be a psychic or a mystic. Whether you think it is cool or is not cool, being psychic only means you are connected with your visions and that you also let them talk to you. Who doesn't want that?

The moon at the Hairline is a time when your dreams can be amazingly powerful. It's a time when you realize you can actually get insights for and about people when you meditate. You get messages which may be for yourself or for other people. It's at this time when it's advisable to write down your dreams. If you're not dreaming, just write down what comes to you in meditation and then have the courage to act on them.

If you are in the challenged aspect of the Hairline, it's no fun because you just feel like nothing is coming. Being challenged, you wouldn't really understand the intuition that comes and why knowingness is blocked. It makes you doubt everything! That's what paranoia is about—you either doubt or fabricate something in your mind. When you get challenged, you get fearful and strangely paranoid. Your intuition closes down and you are disconnected from your visions and dreams.

When you are in your visions, you actually claim them, and you can say, "Okay, this is trying to talk to me." That's actually a good deal because it means you get it! Sometimes, people dream about a future event like an earthquake or some other disaster, but sometimes, they don't trust the dream enough to really tell anybody else about them. It's only after the event had already happened that they say they had the dream. So the Hairline Center allows you to be a visionary; to be familiar with and trust that knowing. That's its positive side.

On the other hand, the negative side of the Hairline, generally a state of paranoia, is really what happens when we feel like we don't have any visions and the world is against us. It is not fun, so we must do what we can to keep ourselves from reaching that level of craziness. The idea is to get balanced in the Hairline. Several things can help you in this area. One of these is bowing. Bowing is so powerful! When you bow, your blood flows into your head and when it courses back down, something magical happens. It changes the energy of the frontal lobe of your brain.

Exercise: To Relax and Release Your Brain

I am going to teach you an exercise that's super simple and you can do this against a wall, on a desk, or on the floor. With the fingertips on a surface, you are going to inhale with the head up and exhale and bring that head in between your hands. If you choose to do this standing, you are also going to open your legs wide and bow with fingertips on the floor. Do this for at least 90 seconds so you can feel what this can do. Three minutes is best. Inhale and then exhale. If your head does not feel clearer, more open, and energized afterwards, then you must do it for a longer time. It can take anywhere between 30 seconds to 3 minutes to totally stimulate your glands. The result of this exercise is that you get out of your paranoid state as quickly as you can bow.

This is a video that shows how to do the exercise. Do it with me for more fun and company. Relaxing and releasing your brain at your desk (VIDEO). You can do this same exercise standing up. You'll feel the "ahhh" factor after doing this, I promise. (The Energy Guru - Stress Buster Brain Clear Video http://youtu.be/ryYS4m-ypS0)

Mantra: Change the Frequency of the Frontal Lobe

There is a mantra exercise where you simply say, "Who la, who la, who la." This sound mantra can change the frequency of your frontal lobe. It's an amazing way to counter Hairline paranoia because it's easy to do when you feel ungrounded.

Exercise: Comb to Consolidate the Energy in Your Crown

Do you realize that the simple act of combing really does more than just fix your hair? We don't have to learn it because we do it naturally. There's a technique to combing for the Hairline. In the morning, you should first comb your hair down and forward before combing upwards and arranging your hair. This is to consolidate the energy in your crown brings all that energy down through your body. It takes only a few seconds. Using a wooden comb or a boar-bristle brush is the best way to fix the magnetic field of your hair. These grooming tools create no static electricity and they massage your scalp at the same time. So even if you can't give yourself a hot oil or scalp treatment, you can still stimulate the Hairline through the basic act of combing or brushing. Your hair is your antenna.

If combing actually nourishes the Hairline, imagine what the right foods can do for it! When it comes to food, you will have to deal with yamas and niyamas, or dos and don'ts. The niyamas are the no nos. Nothing fried or cooked with oils other than ghee, sesame, grape seed, coconut or olive. Frying oil builds up in skin, pores, liver, gallbladder, and even in the glands of your head.

It's good to learn about good oils like flaxseed oil, grape seed oil, olive oil, and ghee, which is a kind of clarified butter. These are really good oils to cook with. Women really need good oils for the lubrication of joints and for radiant skin. But as we are all different, it's best to use oils that work for you. If flax oil works for you, then use it. If it makes you feel fat and cranky, then stop using it. It's that simple. Try making changes one at a time with food to see what works and what doesn't.

Exercise: Sipping Breath to Stimulate the Hairline

Another way to stimulate the Hairline is to use Sipping Breath. To do it, you only have to pretend like there's a straw in your mouth. You breathe in through the mouth and exhale out the nose. Do it with your eyes closed and your hands on your lap. Do this for 3 to 11 minutes (always good guidelines). You will feel good enough to connect with your visions.

The Hairline is a conduit to the infinite where your hair functions as an antenna. It's all about being receptive to energy and allowing this energy to flow into you through certain actions. When you achieve your neutral mind, you utilize your visions, live up to them, use them as your guideposts in life, and you fearlessly deliver them to others with intention.

Empowered in the Hairline

The Hairline is the place where you can be immovable, solid in what you understand to be true and disinterested in any BS. Knowing this, you can proactively use the visions you get and thus close your mouth in time to allow yourself to think first before you speak. Remember, all life is about perceptions. You may not have tons of patience expressing what you feel, so use your mouth with great care and go for kindness even if you feel someone is being ridiculous with you. This is a great time to hang around with others who have great visions and reinforce your belief. Be still and quiet. Through the silence, the visions come through clearly.

Disempowered in the Hairline

When you are disempowered in the Hairline, paranoia dominates the mind. You feel watched and think that no one understands you or your dreams. The best thing to do is to meditate at this time.

Balancing Exercises for the Hairline

Four Part Miracle Breath: Break up those overwhelming feelings and blow your stress away!

Duration: 1-3 minutes

Sit up straight and inhale through the mouth, filling your lungs in four equal parts—starting the breath as low as possible in the abdomen. Exhale through the mouth in four equal parts, from the upper chest down. If you feel relaxed you can do this exercise breathing through the nose. Repeat the cycle.

The Gift:

Instantly reduces stress and see a situation more objectively. Helps dissolve overwhelming feelings.

Three Part Forward Bend: This exercise is something that's effective in moving feelings through you. Doing this properly is the trick to feel less stressed.

Duration: 1-3 minutes

Stand with legs wide open. The stiffer you feel, the wider you should spread the legs. Bend over and place the fingertips on the floor right under the shoulders. Bend the knees if necessary. When inhaling, lift the trunk and head parallel to the floor. Exhale in three-parts, also lowering head and trunk towards the floor in three equal parts.

The Gift:

This pumping motion activates the spinal fluid up and down the spine and through the brain and allows your legs and spine to stretch. The enhanced breath helps release overwhelming feelings.

Eyebrows

Overview

In the Eyebrows, the moon will produce very healing dreams—both sleeping and waking. You will have visions for yourself and others. Your intuition is very open. If you don't trust this state you will likely go for the cheap substitute of "fantasyland" on all levels. The saying that applies for women in the challenged state of this center is, "When we are in this spot, men can build fantasy castles and we move into them." Sound familiar? To balance this Center, you can use its visionary quality and say goodbye to the fantasies.

The Details

The beauty of your eyebrows is that they are pretty neat looking things. The whole face seems incomplete without them over our eyes. They are both all about healing and protecting. They are like these little window awnings for our eyes.

Dust and all manner of things in the air, including sweat from the brow, are caught by the eyebrows before they reach the eyes.

Eyebrows are also a source of sensory delight. You can feel a snowflake that falls on your forehead, but even when it melts, the drop of water it leaves behind doesn't get in your eye because it's protected by the eyebrow. You can just let it snow on your forehead and your eyebrows will take care of the snowflakes.

Have you noticed how we move our eyebrows without even thinking? When we question something, one eyebrow usually rises even when we're not aware of it. It's like our eyebrows talk for us. Sometimes, you look in the mirror and wonder why your eyebrows look so weird. We do weird things to our eyebrows. We pluck them, we pencil them; we have whole relationships with techniques on getting them to look like what we want.

So what happens in the Eyebrows? The visions that come are about healing. They're about knowing what it is to heal and how to get into healing mode for yourself and others.

This can be really challenging if we don't trust ourselves or the dreams.

Complaining about a lack of time is among the things that women often use as an excuse to do other things. They always say they have things to take care of, but they don't seem to have the time to take care of themselves. That's actually a state of being challenged in the Eyebrows. It's when you're not feeling whole or healed. It's when you don't feel connected with what's real and you feel left out and resort to excuses. You feel very dis-eased, but not in the sense that you often think about disease, but rather there's a total lack of ease in your life. You want to be in a fantasyland because you are out of sync with your life or don't want to face what needs to be healed. This makes you very susceptible to buying into your fantasies and the fantasies of others. The truth of it is that when you are in the vastness of your healing visions, your experience is so much more powerful than any fantasy.

Now you are going to learn some things to get out of your fantasy and into healing so you can actually see what you need to see in your visions. Remember, fantasies are simply someone else's dream; they're not yours. In the Eyebrows, you naturally feel like you already know what to do to heal yourself. Healing is really about knowing how to obey intuition and be in the flow of the infinite. Everybody has a capacity to heal. But there are things that you must do to heal in relation to the Eyebrows Center. The first thing to do is to know and admit what you love. Think. What do you love? Make a list—a love list.

Mantra: Chanting While Walking Meditation

Write down at least three things that you really love doing. Do you love going to the art museum? Do you love reading a book by yourself? These things that you love doing may be more important than sleep sometimes. If you make a list of these before meditating, you are adding to and answering your healing dreams and you will have more energy for everything else that you do and experience in your life.

If you'd rather walk instead of stay in one place meditating, then you can do a walking meditation. Just walk and say, "Sa ta na ma, sa ta na ma, sa ta na ma." Sa means creation, birth, or a coming into life. Ta means life, Na means no, not, or without, Ma means rebirth, re-gifted, or another chance. Sat Nam means "truth is the essence of you" or "the identity of you." When you do the walking meditation, synchronize your movement with this chant.

Life becomes like a lie if you don't live the fullness of your healing dreams. If you don't take care of yourself and don't honor the healing that's possible in your life, you become prone to some disease and then everyone around you will end up either taking care of you or leaving you for fear of catching it. Do you really want this? Do *they* really want that? I don't think so!

There are so many little things that we can do to get our life back and return into the realm of the healing visions so that we can be who we are—as healers.

Mantra: Creating a Powerful Reality

Another method is to use a mantra. If you say a mantra at least three times every hour, whatever that mantra is about will become a reality. So if you say, "I am healed and I am more powerful and better every day" three times for every hour, you will soon experience that reality. In other words, what you say will come true. If you say, "I am more prosperous and loving and giving," you *will* become more prosperous, loving, and giving. That's what the neutral mind does. It takes everything in, synthesizes it, and then creates something really powerful. You should really be careful of what you wish for because our thoughts have real power to change our experience of life.

Yogi Bhajan used to say to me, "Be impersonally personal." This saying is really a reference to your neutral mind. Simply getting involved in fantasies and the emotions associated with them will not solve anything. What you must really want for yourself is a relationship with your neutral mind.

In the Eyebrows Center, a neutral mind will serve you well in the most challenging aspects of your life.

Empowered in the Eyebrows

This is even more visionary than the Hairline but in a more fluid and nebulous way. You won't feel grounded during these days. If you need to be grounded, walk barefoot on grass or in the sand. You can also massage your feet.

Disempowered in the Eyebrows

Here you are very prone to fantasies and to not being present. You are spacey and just want fulfillment in fantasies because you are not happy with your life. It's most unfortunate if you only find fulfillment in fantasy. I said *most unfortunate* because that will only lead you into addictive patterns and get you into trouble. The fantasy will own you. It will never really give you true fulfillment. Do the recommended exercises and move your body. Do yoga, martial arts, hard workouts, and extreme sports. Let your flimsy fantasy meet solid earth. This will definitely bring you back to you.

Balancing Exercise for the Eyebrows

Heel Pounding: Walk on the wise side.

Duration: 30-60 seconds on each foot

Remove both of your shoes. Make a fist with your right hand and pound on your right heel. Then you switch to your left hand and left foot. You can use cold water on your feet as you do this as this awakens all the thousands of nerve endings in the feet. Eat root veggies and heavier foods like beans and a grain. Do not eat meat as this will interfere with the visions. Also, you must not drink any alcoholic beverages during this time.

The Gift:

The activation of powerful nerve endings has a calming effect on your brain. It helps balance the brain and emotional states. It's useful in breaking children's tantrums.

Cheeks

Overview

The moon in the Cheeks makes you ready to do PR for anyone and everyone. This is a great time to network, when you feel very bright and radiant. People may tell you how beautiful you look. This is actually the light shining out from you that is attractive. However, when you are challenged, it is out of control flirting. There's the urge to look for someone to mirror back to you that you are good, beautiful, and fabulous instead of you knowing and owning those assets.

The Cheeks are a really great Moon Center. I love it because it's all about who we are as women. Its domain is vast and covers a big part of the face. We are always doing stuff to our cheeks, like we make them stand out to look redder, higher, and tighter by putting blush on them. We love to kiss children's cheeks because they are so soft and yummy. We simply love our cheeks!

When in the positive aspect of the Cheeks Center, you become a PR magnate.

You get the capacity to promote and make things happen without effort. You can easily think of something to promote for someone or make something better. It can be anything from fundraising in school to a new way to advertise a business. Like, instead of having your kids sell magazines, candy, and other trivial stuff in school, you can help the school procure other things to sell that matter, like aromatherapy oils and candles. In the Cheeks Center, everything easily falls into place concerning promotion. You actually see an idea and know exactly how to promote it!

At one time, I watched a group of women in London while we were out for dinner. One woman took out a brochure for an event she was doing. Another woman looked at this brochure and commented on how good the brochure was, except for a few things that needed to be changed. She went through the brochure correcting things just as easily as she would count. Obviously she had her Cheeks Center on her side because she was so right on. The brochure designer was so pleased with the corrections, she honestly appreciated every comment the other woman gave her. Through the Cheeks, the woman was able to take PR to a whole new realm. She came across as very secure, uplifted, radiant, and powerful!

It's very much the opposite when you are challenged in the Cheeks, where you doubt everything you do and flirt with everyone just to get their positive feedback. Flirting is just promoting oneself without any kind of sustained belief in yourself. Flirting is like saying, "Tell me that I am beautiful and that I am worthy. That you want me!" That's really what flirting is about. Ultimately, flirting means you want others to tell you that you are wonderful and that you are whatever it is they want. It's not you who's giving praise or feeding that part of yourself.

Perhaps the best way to get neutral in the Cheeks is to take radiant foods, like alkaline produce. What kinds of food are alkaline? Well, fruits, vegetables, some nuts (almonds and walnuts), and grains like quinoa, amaranth, millet, long grain brown rice and kasha are the foods that will make you feel radiant. Eating nuts and legumes may sound like the most boring thing in the world, but it's so exciting because you feel good and alive with radiant energy after you eat them and you can make them taste like anything you desire. There are such amazingly wonderful nut paté recipes everywhere. Raw food cookbooks are the best places to look. Beans, quinoa, millet, and amaranth are wonderful and taste so good you can add them to almost anything you can eat. I mix these grains in my salad all the time!

Recipe: Sautéed Ginger and Almonds for Menstrual Cramps

For women, radiant food can mean different things for different times of the month. Eggplant is good a couple weeks before your period. (look at the shape of the fruit or veggie and it gives you a clue to its gifts) On your cycle, a really good thing to eat is ginger and almonds.

Take a skillet and use Ghee or good cooking oil. Coconut oil is best used here for good taste. Heat it, then take a piece of ginger about 1-2 inches long and slice it really thinly. Add this to the hot oil, then, add the almonds with the skins on and start sautéing dry or with just a little oil. Take the sautéed ginger and almonds off the stove and allow tem to cool. Pour some raw honey over them. It's almost like almond/ginger brittle—tasty and delicious! The ginger helps ease menstrual cramps and aids in digestion due to the high calcium and magnesium. Almonds help with the body's mineral balance which tends to go a little wonky on your cycle. This recipe serves to balance energy in your body and mind.

Recipe: Quinoa Pasta with a Cilantro-Parsley Pesto

Now here's a recipe for something that's really lovely and that I love to make. It's called quinoa pasta with a cilantro-parsley pesto. I use lemon, olive oil, parsley, cilantro, salt, and pepper all blended together. You can add garlic if you wish. It is so simple and delicious you can eat it like you would pesto. You can put it on top of some pasta if you want, eat it with crackers, or use it as a dip. It's really fabulous! It's so nourishing by itself, but if you really want it to be super nourishing, put in half an avocado. All those greens and minerals in this recipe will make your life bright! I must tell you I don't measure when I cook, so all ingredients in my recipes are approximations. To be sure that you're doing it right, simply add to it and taste if you need to.

Yummy Cilantro-Parsley Pesto Recipe

1 bunch of parsley *and*
1 bunch of cilantro (I like an even
    blend; if you like one more, use
    less of the other)
1 tsp of sea salt
1 tsp of black pepper
1 half lemon, or depending on how
    juicy you want it
1/2 cup to 3/4 cup olive oil
Water, enough to blend

You can make it more watery or oily for a sauce, or thicker, and it makes a great dip. You can even substitute arugula for the parsley and cilantro.

It's important to be aware of what you're putting into your body and to take good care of it. It's like a car that eventually runs down without enough fuel and proper maintenance. What would happen if you let your car always run out of gas or never took it in for check-ups? Of course it would soon be belching and freaking out on you. We can also do that to ourselves if we go low on radiant food and feed ourselves junk. Twinkies, sweet and salty foods, fried foods, and all other kinds of junk food can make you feel hideous. What you put in the tank is how you are going to feel. You are what you eat, so make each meal count. The most important meal of the day is the meal that really counts for you and it's not necessarily breakfast.

There was this time when I went to London from Canada. By the wonders of modern travel, I was whisked to a totally different time zone just like that. My timing was so off and I was hungry in the morning even though I rarely eat breakfast. So I ate a whole bag of nuts and fruit. The people with me hardly had anything at all and they just had tea together. They said, "No, we don't eat until noon." So later, they had a really, really big lunch which felt good to them, and I thought: *Oh, good for you!* They listened to their body, and that's what was important.

It truly is important to understand the needs of your body. If you feel you only need to eat five little meals a day or just one big meal, then, do it! Listen to your body to know for sure what it needs to be fed well. If you consume sugar, caffeine and sodas, your body won't talk to you. It will be mad and very busy trying to recover from your abuse. You won't be able to get up and get going if you want to. Please don't cover up your intuition with junk food.

Yoga exercises would really benefit you, especially when you are in the challenged state of any Moon Center. My yoga DVDs are really great and can be very helpful for you! Yogi Bhajan himself told me to make them. Many people have shared their comments about how amazing and helpful these DVDs are. You can find more details about them here - http://gurutej.com/store/kundalini-yoga-dvds/

If you cannot do yoga for the time being, you can do something else, but be sure it makes you perspire abundantly. Women especially need to sweat every day to know they have exercised enough. Exercise makes you radiant and detoxified through the largest detox organ... your skin.

Exercise: For Body Radiance

Go out there and move until you sweat. You can run, row, swim, play tennis, or just do whatever it is you love to do. If you love belly dancing, then go belly dancing! If you're into ballroom dancing, then go ballroom dancing! Move your body for at least 40 minutes. When you come back to your house, you will be all aglow, and that's really what you want to achieve. This is really important because when you feel this way, your radiance extends to everyone around you.

In order to be radiant, you really need to exercise every day even if you can't seem to find the time to do it even twice a week. Doing something every day is sufficient. Try to find something you can do, that you enjoy doing; then it will be easier for you to find the time and the will to exercise more. I love rollerblading because all I have to do is put the skates on, go outside, and roll! That way, I get 40 minutes of exercise and fun!

To benefit from exercise, all you have to do is pop in the The Moon She Rocks You videos that you can download digitally and do some of the exercises you can find there. (http://gurutej.com/store/11-moon-centers/) You may feel you can't make it through the whole thing or even last 40 minutes, but once you do them, you will really feel vibrant, inspired, and energetic. After exercising, always nourish your body with liquids that will reinforce the radiance you gain! It helps to know the liquids that you should and should not drink.

I want to share this story. There was this woman who felt sick. She went to a clinic but the doctor couldn't find anything wrong with her. She got sicker and sicker as time went by and the doctors gave her only three months to live. "We don't know what to do with you," her doctors said, so she decided to take this trip around the world, which the doctors agreed to even if she'd be in a wheelchair. What they didn't know was that the woman was a soda drinker. She drank soda from the time she woke up in the morning. She'd drink soda throughout the day like she would water.

In fact, she hardly drank any pure water at all. She'd drink soda ten times a day!

Now the woman's sister happened to watch something on PBS about the disastrous health effects of all of the ingredients in soda like sugar, caffeine, etc., which make us crazy. The message of the documentary was simple: if people would just stop drinking sodas, they would be healthier.

After listening to this she called up her ailing sister. "Do you have a can of soda open?" she asked. Her sister answered, yes. "I want you to throw it away and never drink another one," she advised. The dying woman refused. The sister answered, "What if I told you that if you stop drinking soda, you can have a life doing everything you want and not die in three months? Would you be willing to stop then?"

Though hesitant, her sister agreed and continued her trip around the world. After three months, she came back from her trip and walked into the doctor's office unaided. "You're not sick anymore?" The doctor asked. "What did you do to get well?" She answered,

"I stopped drinking soda!" That was the only thing she changed.

I need to emphasize that soda will make you sick. Watch DVDs like *Forks over Knives* or *Super Size Me* if you have any doubts about this. Many of us grab what we love to eat and we don't want any research data telling us it is not good for us. I don't want you obsessing about a product that is not good for you; I want you to gravitate to what will support you—the real essence of you.

I could go on and on about sodas, and especially diet sodas containing Aspartame, that artificial sweetener that never leaves your body, and sugar, which is so hard on your nervous system, it makes you depressed and put on weight. But what I really want to do it give you good ideas of how you can move towards that which will support you long-term and not take you down.

Recipe: Sweet Drink Alternative

If you like sweet drinks, try this healthful alternative. Take your favorite organic juice and dilute it with plain water or sparkling water. Voila! For an added immune booster, add a Vitamin C pack. It tastes so great, plus you get lots of Vitamin C. Each fruit has its own unique healing properties. For instance, unsweetened cranberry is quite good for the kidneys and black cherry is great served hot to help with sleep, and it's also good for the liver.

Tea, like Yogi Tea, is another great substitute for sugared drinks. It has body, tastes great, and you can drink it black or add your choice of milk substitute like almond milk, coconut milk, rice milk, soya milk, and others. It's so easy and fun to try new preparations like these and then you can share them with others.

Children often love making new concoctions. It helps to get them to drink or eat what's good for them if they have created it themselves! In trying out new things, make it fun. Go after the new and the old will leave you.

Did you know that there are more than 100 different kinds of tea and that they all have fine healing components? Ninety-nine percent of them taste really good, so it should be easy to get into the groove of drinking tea. To get this habit, start bringing tea bags with you to work. You can even introduce your co-workers to drinking tea. Afterwards, you can organize a tea club where everybody brings in their favorite teas and share them with each other. You'd be surprised at how open people are when drinking tea. I pulled out a tea bag at a family function and everyone wanted to try it. Even the kids loved it! One person said, "I'm buying this tomorrow. Tell me what it is." But remember, this is not an excuse for you to use sugar. Add a touch of honey, agave, or stevia, but see that big red line across sugar or Aspartame.

So please let go of the soda! Make it vanish from your life. You will be stronger, more radiant, and more emotionally balanced. While you can wean yourself away from soda a step at a time, it's best to let go of it now. Step away, throw it away, stay away! You will feel so much better by drinking tea or unsweetened fruit juices instead of soda. Sweet does not always mean good. Water is tasteless, but it's good. We should not allow our tongue to rule. Taste buds change in time.

If you crave sweet food, you must always consider the amount and the quality. If you really want something that's both good and sweet, there's fruit, gluten-free cookies, and organic chocolate that are really low in sugar. Just take a bite or two to get your fix. A nice organic bar that has raw sugar or sweetened fruit juice is very different from a Mars bar not only in taste but also in what it does to your body and mind.

Just know that when you crave sugar it may mean your minerals are low. You should have good sources of sugar and liquid minerals handy. These will keep you from getting tempted by bad sweets that are so easily bought these days from vending machines and *connivence* stores which as sprouting everywhere like toxic mushrooms.

Usually, a sweet craving means you have a mineral deficiency. Liquid minerals can help in this case. Just add them to your drink in the morning in addition to your preferred protein powder (I suggest Sun Warrior Rice protein) and greens. Taking liquid minerals is a great way to start your day without having breakfast and still be radiant!

When you're radiant, you naturally enter the neutral aspect of the Cheeks and you become empowered. So, do everything that you can do to create that radiance. Exercise! Eat well! Drink good liquids that support good health. This is how you will live well and make the most of the gift of this Moon Center so you can be empowered in it.

Empowered in the Cheeks

When you are empowered in the Cheeks, you are a powerful force and can accomplish things in record time. You can do anything for yourself and anyone who asks. You are brilliant and alive, but you must make sure not to burn yourself out, and as they say, burn the candle at both ends. Simply enjoy and breathe life into what you are able to do in this time.

Disempowered in the Cheeks

You flirt with everyone and everything, trying to find the nod, approval, and acknowledgement from the outside in, instead of the other way around. In this time, you should watch yourself and become the observer to find your sense of humor. When you know these days are ahead, get a friend to help remind you of who you really are so you don't fall into a pattern of believing the illusion is real.

Balancing Exercise for the Cheeks

Cheer for the Self: Empower yourself and be your own cheerleader

Duration: 2-3 minutes

Standing on tiptoes, extend the arms up above the shoulders with hands and eyes wide open. Say, "Sa". Next, squat as you swing your arms down. Close your eyes and say "Ta". Then go to a standing position with eyes and hands wide open, and swing your arms to cross in front of chest. Say, "Na." Now remain standing in place and swing your arms back with your elbows bent to your sides. With hands and eyes closed shut as you say, "Ma". Repeat the cycle. It's empowering!

The Gift:

This exercise strengthens your magnetic field and helps reinstate power in who you truly are.

The Energy Guru - Cheer For the Self video http://youtu.be/F9RAKqblP_o.

Lips

Overview

What happens when the moon is in this point? You become talkative—very talkative! You have great verbal and communication skills at this time. Wouldn't it be nice if you could be in this cycle for every presentation you have? In the Lips, you have the desire to communicate the highest goals, so this is not just about being talkative to hear yourself talk. People easily profit from your conscious communication in this Moon Center. When challenged here, you get sharp tongued. That's the forked tongue effect where you have no patience or control of how you say things.

The Details

The Lips Moon Center is all about communication. Your lips, being the soft gates of your beautiful mouth, are needed for you to be able to talk, and you know how those beautiful and fabulous lips can get talkative! You get very, very, very talkative when in the

Lips Center. Now this can be either good or bad as there are pros and cons when in the Lips.

Let's not get ahead of ourselves. What is the Lips Center about? When you are in the Lips, you feel like you can talk about anything. If somebody gives you a topic, you can talk about it like you're an expert no matter what it is. Now it's the opposite in the challenged aspect when you feel like you just can't communicate about anything and you feel stuck in muck, completely incapable of saying anything right, and it's like all you can say is, "I don't know!" It's when you fail to connect with people even when they're right in front of you. This is unlike the neutral aspect of the Center when you naturally connect and talk to them about so many things, even the little miracles all around us that hardly get noticed.

We can talk about many things with others, but it's the little everyday miracles that matter when communicating. I often speak about my experiences with everyday miracles even if they are by no means grand. I talk to others about the hummingbird I saw feeding on a dangling flower and the splash of colorful sunshine I saw through the morning dew. You can talk about anything when in the Lips Center—even about the simple act of breathing. Now breathing is one miracle that people are not aware of. Although it's one of the spontaneous autonomic functions of our body (we don't have to think in order to breathe), we can actually control it at will. Breathing relates to the Lips. Just as you can control your breathing to be deep or shallow, you can also control the depth and vastness of your conversations, courtesy of this Center.

Sometimes, you can talk very deeply when you are in a challenged aspect of your life. In this state, I often talk about how things happen according to a divine plan. Now, you can either choose to be humble or keep on scolding God for letting such horrible things happen to you or you can try to get inside the bigger plan that is. Being vast, deep, and conscious of a divine plan doesn't mean you won't feel sad, but you can use the power of the Lips to talk yourself out of the victim role, and change your frequency about the reality of the situation. If it is happening, it is meant to happen.

Reality is simply how we perceive existence and how we express it through the Lips Center. Reality isn't fixed. It can be changed at any given moment. What we consider reality at this moment is not the same as 5 minutes or two days ago. Our perception can be vast, but what we process and talk about while in the neutral aspect of this Center is vaster, and allows our conversations to become delightful, powerful, and more focused on what really matters.

Yogi Bhajan always encouraged his students to uplift others in their speech. This immediately eliminates the gossip factor. If you haven't noticed, there is really zero uplifting in gossip as not one good thing is said about the person concerned. Even if you say one good thing to cover all the bad, what's in the package remains the same—it still stinks, only it's wrapped in something that makes it look good. You cannot cover up crap with chocolate and call it candy!

Think before you speak. It is easy for us to say really mean things like, "Wow you must have had a really late night" when we could instead say, "If you need any help today let me know. I know what it's like to be tired." More often than not, we slice, dice, and tear people apart. But we've always had the choice to use words in a creative and mending way. Why not make use of that choice?

I'd like to share a really wonderful thing that someone once told me. He said, "Don't talk to anyone in a way that you yourself wouldn't like from someone when in your most delicate state." Does that make sense? How would you like to be talked to in a mean manner when in your most sensitive time? So talk to everyone as if they mattered, because they do! Talk to people like they're a part of you, because they are! You may not realize it, but what you say to others now can mean a lot to them later on.

I've had people come back ten, twenty, thirty, even forty years later and tell me things I had said that impacted their lives and changed them forever. I never knew it then, but in those times, I was just saying what needed to be said. The fact is that words by themselves are powerful! Use them in the wrong way and they can take somebody's life apart. A friend of mine says, "Your tongue is a pen." One of my students said, "True and you can't suck the ink back."

On the other hand, words can uplift and give people reassurance and hope. When you feel that catty bitch coming, take a really deep breath. Inhale through your mouth and exhale through the nostrils. Do this five times and you will feel yourself calming down. If five times is not enough, then do a few more. Great releaser! Also try Dragon Breath, you will love this one.

All of these breaths offered have the capacity to change the frequency of your brain and realign it to calm and neutral mode. Use them often and you will experience a more fulfilling life every day as you interact and communicate with other people.

Break Breath

This is the best kept secret yet. Break Breath is for breaking up overwhelming emotions in you. You break your breath into 4 segments or sips. This breaks down what seems to be looming large in your life. This breath is for anger, frustration, upset.

Inhale in 4 parts, sipping the breath in through the mouth. The eyes can be closed if possible. On the exhale you will stick your tongue out as far as possible and open your eyes super wide. You may laugh. Continue to do this at least 5 more times.

Opening the eyes super wide activates your intuition. The tongue put out balances your parathyroid gland. Children love this. Do this in the midst of a fight and poof, end of fight. Humor will save the day. Or do it in front of a mirror when taking yourself too seriously.

Mantra: Balance the Pituitary

By itself, breathing is very useful, but use a mantra with it and you get results that transform you. It's the double shot of power. Now all mantras are really fabulous, but one that really works with the Lips is, "Ma ma ma ma ma." This mantra helps to balance your pituitary, which is a master gland. It also gets the lips moving and helps you find the capacity to use words to give people another chance, a new life; a rebirth, instead of a putdown. We are going to say this in two ways. Here's one version:

"Ma ma ma ma ma ma ma ma ma ma ma ma ma ma ma ma ma ma!" Do this in a staccato and quickly.

If you say this continuously for five minutes I promise you, you won't have another funky thing to say about anybody because your mouth will be so alive and your third eye will be so open that you will see things totally differently.

Now the other version needs a longer ma, so say, "Mmmmmaaaaaaa!" Make sure the M is really long. You want to vibrate your lips effectively well by holding the M longer. "Mmmmmmmmaaaaaaaaaaaa!" Do it again, "Mmmmmmmmaaaaaaaaaaaaa!" Reading a mantra and imagining how it's spoken is one thing, but actually listening to the mantra as the sound is made by your lips is another thing. Do it and listen to it carefully. Be guided. Remember, all these are in the DVD series.

Recipes: For Cooling and Warming the Body

Let's talk now about food for the Lips Center. Have you have ever noticed that when you dislike somebody you have a sharp tongue, agitated, and are hot under the collar? To counteract this state, you need something cool, but that doesn't mean we have to take ice. When you are really agitated, you can take a breath—Sitali for cooling and Breath of Fire to bring up the heat.

Sitali is inhaling through a rolled tongue with the tip of the tongue extended out past the lips. Exhale through the nose. Do this for 3 min.

Breath of Fire is a rapid, continuous, and diaphragmatic breath that can be done laying down, sitting up, or walking for 3min.

Juices

Pick a really good juicer (not a blender, which is great for raw soups but not for juicing). A mix of cucumber and celery juice is perfect for cooling. If you want more heat, then beets are perfect. But you must consider a few guidelines because one thing about beet is that its juice is so concentrated. You should only mix beet with some other kind of juice. When using beet, never make it more than 1/3 of your juice. You wouldn't want to drink beet juice straight! You can do beet and apple, or beet and apple and ginger (ginger is very heat producing); you can even do carrot and beet if you want to. If you want to get rid of heat in the body, do not add ginger. Ginger creates more heat, so it's not a good thing to drink when you're agitated, but it is great when you need energy.

There are so many juices and they all have so many uses. They are all so good! If you are familiar with juices and their nutritional values, you will know what fruit and vegetable juices to take and when to take them. My favorite juices are lemon, ginger, and apple or green juices. Many fruits and vegetable juices work to cool the Lips Center when it's hot.

Melons, cucumbers, and celery are very cooling and come in handy when your lips get too hot to handle. Cucumber and celery go well together and you can add lemon for a triple cooling combination. To calm anger, frustration, and balance the liver, there's beet, radish, and carrot. It's sweet, so add some lemon for tartness. For those who crave sweets, this apple, lemon, and ginger combo is yummy, very alkaline and good for the gall bladder. Mixing in more apple gives more sweetness; adding more ginger wakes you up; adding lemon helps get you out of the dumps and provides zest and energy for life. Extra garlic in any juice will clean your digestive system. Adding ginger will heat up the body, which works especially well for thin people. Ginger and garlic (as well as onion) can help men produce more semen. In any juice, you can add potato, blueberry, cherry, strawberry, and other low glycemic fruits that are yummy and rich in phyto-nutrients. These sweets won't throw your sugars out of whack and make you more emotional. It's always good to know your juices!

There's a saying from the 60s, "Drink your food and eat your juice." It means that when you drink fresh juice, you should swish it around in your mouth like a great cognac (I used to drink but stopped before turning legal) and drink it slowly so that you get the benefit of the enzymes. To get the most out of solid food, you must chew it a hundred times before swallowing. Either way, it's like you're extracting the very juices that contain the nourishment you need from food.

If you don't have the right juices or food to fix you up, then you can simply think of things that will either warm you up or cool you down. Thinking of something cooling has the same effect as eating cooling fruits and vegetables. The mere thought of cooling things will make you feel cooler and calmer. This kind of physiological effect comes from that connection of the Lips.

We could go on and on but I only want to give some guidelines here. Play with this. Find the kind of nourishment that you like and ones that like you back. Know the ones that make you feel great, kind, and expansive. Using this method, you can speak calmly even while challenged in the Lips.

To be connected to the heart is to hear it speak to you. When your heart starts to thump strongly in your chest, it is saying, "Stop it this instant!" It is telling you to stop whatever it is that's coming out between your lips so that you won't be slicing and dicing anybody with your words—you would simply be expressing yourself.

Now what exercises are right for the Lips? Well, they are the ones that allow you to say a mantra. Remember that when you exercise, the most important thing is your focus and this is reached with the help of the sound current you are creating while you are doing the exercise. People can be so busy even when it is counter indicated. When they are on their bike exercising, for example, they might also be watching television and effectively distracting themselves as opposed to attracting themselves.

When you have a mantra, you can play with it and you can change the focus of your mind with that sound. It's like when you hear a bird's song and you focus on it and say, "Oh, my God, listen to that wonderful song!" There's this wholly beautiful interaction between you and others that is all about finding your voice and utilizing that voice properly so that your communion with other people becomes sacred. I have mentioned before how I skate through the neighborhood chanting. So, let me say again—skating while chanting a mantra is a wonderful thing to do. I heal both myself and the neighborhood! Here is a super simple mantra. "I like myself. I love myself. I see my soul." Do this one three times an hour and see what happens. Do this when you exercise. This is the time to use your eagerness to talk and to be heard; to uplift yourself.

Exercise: Kiss the Heart by Kissing the Center of the Hand

Now there is one exercise that's really quite fun and you don't need to go anywhere to do it. You just lie down on your back or sit up. All you do is kiss the center of your hand. Make the kiss really slurpy and juicy. Do this for three to five minutes. By kissing the center of your hand, you are, in effect, also kissing the heart.

Exercise: Bringing Heaven and Earth Together

There is another exercise you can do while you are on your back. You bring your leg up and kiss your knee, switching back and forth from one side to the other. By bringing the knee and the head up to a kiss, you bring heaven and earth together to create paradise!

The Moon She Rocks You

By giving attention to the Lips Center, you can be aware and truly grateful as to how these lips serve you. They help you speak and communicate truthfully; they are there to kiss and be kissed; they are a necessary part of forming all words. It's so easy to talk about a rose but it is not so easy to talk about the infinity of its creation and destruction. God is constantly generating, organizing, and also destroying everything in this cycle. We tend to hate the destruction and totally ignore it in favor of the creation part, but no matter what our preferences are, it's all God's doing. There is really nothing that's not about God.

We need to see things from a different perspective. We already know how good our lips are for French kissing, but we also need to see how they are really good at forming words that remain forever in existence. Honor and be grateful for your lips.

Sometimes people can make you feel puny and depressed in your Lips Center. When you feel challenged by another person, first close your lips then say: "No! Not going to react! Need to understand first and then deal with the situation. I'm taking a break breath first." Now, there's no guarantee that every communication between you and another person is going to be perfect when you apply this coping method, but you'll certainly get a better outcome than usual. If you slow down, take two steps back, and look at the scenario from higher ground, you'll see the reason why you shouldn't react negatively. Words have the power to encourage people to make the changes they need to make to unlock the gifts of the Lips Center. Through the lips, words are given a real voice.

If you knew that every word you said would truly impact on people and be recorded for all eternity, how would you speak? Our words are all out there for the entire universe to hear. You can't take them back once you've spoken them. One way to be more conscious of what you say is use things that interrupt you when you start to say something you would normally regret later on. These "interrupters" will keep you from walking into the bad neighborhood of the Lips.

A really great interrupter is water. Take a long drink of water when you feel your lips going bad. By the time you are finished taking it all in, you will feel and see things differently. You can get cranky because you've not had enough water. That happens to most of us. So drink a lot of water and be grateful that there's still water around to drink! You can use water as an interrupter whenever you feel that you're going into that negative place. The voice that goes through those lips of yours is super important! Give it the attention it needs.

Empowered in the Lips

Here in this Moon Center, you are on top of your verbal communications. Being empowered in this Moon Center means you truly become the great communicator that you are. The right words will just flow out.

Disempowered in the Lips

This is when you can really rip someone apart to shreds. Watch your tongue when challenged. Better still, zip your mouth for two days. Silence is a great tool, it will serve you well in this Center. Listen to yourself internally and lose the judgment. This will help shift the gears of your Lips Center towards empowerment.

Balancing Exercises for the Lips

Chanting la la la: You need to use our tongue and lips for this chant. This exercise is done in a continuous tone.

Duration: 2-3 minutes at least

Another great and easy thing is to run your tongue around the outside of your teeth and gums.

The Gift:

This works on the meridians to balance your brain and for you to connect to the heart in your communications.

Chanting La, la, la with Wide Open Mouth: This exercise is done with the mouth wide open.

Duration: 3 minutes

Chant La, la, la with the mouth wide open and using only the tip of the tongue.

The Moon She Rocks You

The Gift:

The use of the muscles in your tongue brings new awareness.

Earlobes

Overview

The Earlobes Moon Center is where you want to discuss the depth of why you are here on this planet and what you stand for. Your values and principles are the topics. In this Center, you want to be around those who will connect with you at this level of depth. Challenged, it turns on you and you analyze everything you think, do, say, and imagine. This can be good when introspective but not when self-deprecating.

The Details

Ah, the Earlobes Moon Center! What would we do without it? In the positive aspect of this Center, you want to discuss your life, what's happening in it, and what you want to happen with it in the future.

We love to stick things through our earlobes. Beautiful ornaments like earrings can be irresistible to women, but they are very sensitive, those earlobes of yours. Ask any acupuncturist if it's a really good idea to keep sticking a needle through the ears in the same place and they'd shake their head. I remember Yogi Bhajan telling us, "Do not put anything in your earlobes on a regular basis unless it is a full carat diamond." Yes, that's right, a full carat diamond! That's something of real value. The diamond has clarity of vibration. It's the only thing that does not blow all those sensitive acupuncture points with continuous stimulation. Think about it, valuable earrings are often passed down from one generation to the next before they are given to you and end up in your earlobes. So the Earlobes Center is all about values. Your earlobes stand for your values and the foundations of your life.

When you are neutral in this Center, you can talk about the things you value. In most cases, you want to re-evaluate all your relationships and the situations in your life and you tend to ask questions like: Are we on the same page? Do we still want the same things that we valued in the past? Are we on track with what we said we wanted to do? These questions are pretty common when you are in your Earlobes Center. In the neutral there is no question in your mind about what you need to do. It's like you can say with certainty, "This is what I stand for and if it means everything falls away from me, so be it!"

The people who actually know their values and what they are willing to die for are the people we usually admire. They are the ones who do whatever it takes to spread those values so other people have the opportunity to live them.

It doesn't matter if it means going all the way to Africa and feeding starving children. It doesn't matter if it means becoming that person in the neighborhood who starts running an after-school reading program for children. It doesn't matter if it's working in social shelters to help abused women get back on track or run for public office. Their resolution means they know their life has value and it's far greater than what they've done thus far in life. Do you have an inkling of what you stand for?

In the challenged aspect of the Earlobes Moon Center, it's likely you will be asking a different set of questions or enter a confused state and say something like, "I have no idea what I am doing!" or "I don't know what this job is about!" You will question everything you encounter and you will feel really disconnected and disheartened. You may be very self-deprecating and feel you should be doing this or that, but you can't make yourself do it. It's like you have all these paths to choose from but you can't pick the right one. You feel stupid, worthless, and quite turned against your own self. You talk to yourself, but this internal talk is not uplifting. It's self-deprecating, and that means there is no self-love. You feel really bad about how you are living your life, inside and out. Nonetheless, being challenged in the Earlobes also makes you very funny. Comedians know this more than anyone else. They know how to use self-deprecation as a tool for making people laugh. Unfortunately, people can't take you seriously if you're often in this state. They would only see you as a funny person and not someone who can change the world. The great thing about the Earlobes Center is that it cycles every 28 days, which means that in that cycle, it's a really good thing to re-evaluate the connectivity between what you believe and what you know, so you can adjust accordingly.

It matters how you live your life. You only have to take a look at how you are living it within the confines of your body. You see, our body is the housing unit of our spirit and it is fabulous no matter how small or confining you think it is! The Earlobes Center coaxes you to look deeply into your unit, where your spirit lies, making you become aware of what you're really doing with your life and whether it coincides with what you thought you were actually meant to be or do. You feel confined when your life is not aligned with what your essence—your spirit—wants you to do.

Ask kids what they want to be when they grow up and the boys usually all say, I want to be a fireman, fly planes, or be an astronaut. The girls, on the other hand, usually want to be a mommy, a teacher, a dancer, or a business owner. They know what they want to be! Unlike kids who look forward, we adults look at what we've evolved into, and we make very conscious, or more often unconscious decisions about the way we want to present ourselves in the world. This may or may not be aligned with the wishes of our spirit.

Undecided, we sometimes let ourselves be washed up on a shore hoping destiny will take us where we're needed. It's like when something comes up and you can't decide whether to act on it or not. You switch back and forth, leaning first one way, and then the other. Some people easily get to high places by just allowing things to happen. But if they don't learn along the way they won't stay in those higher places by their own deeds. This is the time to make your deeds and your values aligned.

When we don't feel aligned to our values, we want to get away from ourselves. We act in a way that makes everybody else want to get away from us too. Even when we appear content with where we are and what we've done. We get really snarky and weird because we are trying to push everybody away. We don't want them to see who we really are because we don't know our own self. It's either that or we are not willing to look at the disharmony. Once you get a good look at what's off with you, then you have the capacity to change it. Sometimes, though, you may think it's too painful to face. This very avoidance disconnects you from what's important. Distractors like television, emails, and YouTube become our escape.

Can you imagine if a train's cars were not connected well to each other and then the train went quickly around a bend? All the compartments would just fly right off the track! That's exactly what happens to you when you don't have the right words to admit that you're off track. Fortunately, you can use the gift of the Earlobes Center to bring yourself right back into the groove with your spirit and your true purpose in life. To benefit from that gift, to get your life going on the right track, you only need to do a few simple things.

Sometimes we fail to notice that the things we eat affect our lives in many ways. If you have gluten intolerance, you can't eat wheat, corn, or things that even have traces of glutinous products without feeling hideous. You can see labeling on products now that list if they come from factories that pack glutinous products or nuts. If you are prone to Candida, which is a yeast infection that can make you bloated after meals, have headaches, and feel really tired and miserable, you must avoid anything with sugars—even fruit—and nothing that is fermented, except sauerkraut. Take nothing that breaks down into sugars quickly. With Candida, you should be eating brown rice, quinoa, lots of vegetables, garlic, and olive oil. For every disease that is in your body, there are things that you must eat and there are things you must not eat. Knowing your weaknesses and working with those instead of ignoring and trying to override them is what this center is about.

In choosing food to eat, you must ask a few essential food value questions: Does it taste good? How good is it for me? Is it going to empower me so I can do what I need to do? Is it going to make me groggy and tired, thick and dumb, or somewhere in-between? Just imagine you have a life force value meter with a range of 1 to 100 and that every time you want something to eat, you look at the reading on this life force meter. It's like that halo that you see on saints and gurus, which you also have, by the way, even if you're not aware of it. It serves as your life force meter with 100 being the best reading. This imaginary meter is useful when it comes to food.

Your food choices must start when you make your shopping list. It does not start when you put things in your mouth. The things that you shop for and buy are what you will have around and inside of you for a long time. So make sure that when you make that shopping list, you do it from a true value point of view. The value of an item should be based on how useful it is to you. You must not measure value based on others' opinion, like how much your children are going to badger you if you don't buy them what they want or how much your partner is going to whine if something he likes is not available. You've probably heard of getting good value when shopping for your family, but what value is being spoken of, really? Not just the money aspect. For food, it can be a lot of things. Is it organic? How deeply will it nourish your family? Is it appealing to the taste buds? Picking food is like exchanging wonderful recipes with friends. You know a recipe has value if it's quick and nutritious. So is your shopping for it.

I'm partial to this amazing cleanse that is simply called The Cleanse of Sta. Fe (http://thecleanse.com). It's an 11-day cleanse and it gets people into a highly alkalized diet. If you do this and the follow up for 40 days, you can get into a great eating habit. 11 days isn't really a whole habit breaker but it's enough time for an experience. I have had so many people who did this cleanse at least once in their life and afterwards, they say they can literally see better, smell better, and hear better. It's like they have their senses opened up for the first time.

This cleanse is also a commitment to learning how to cook differently and eat differently. But then without a commitment, many people go back to their old way of eating even after they felt really good because of this cleanse. If you do the 40 days extension however, it can really stick with you. It's really more than just getting results, though—it's about valuing the experience and translating it as a part of your life. I really recommend this cleanse. You can find out more about this special cleanse in the complete The Moon She Rocks You video program series. (http://gurutej.com/store/11-moon-centers/)

All you need to do to get value from what you eat is to sit down and be with your food. If you are not sitting down at the table and being conscious of your food, then it is super easy to overeat or eat "snacks" that are not good for you. You need to be present and to check in with yourself before you can be conscious about what you are doing. If you think and say, "I am what I eat," then you will get a realization that will make you ultimately change what you eat for the better. If you have kids, it's best to teach them about food, otherwise they will learn from other people about things that may not really be good for them.

I was already 60 before I heard of putting M&Ms in popcorn, melting them and eating them. I have been told by people stories of what they did as kids and they'd recall with much enthusiasm, "Oh, yeah! We used to put M&Ms in hot popcorn and when the chocolate melts all over them, you get peanuts and popcorn that are all clumped together, which is so good and fun to eat." I thought, Oh, my God! I am so blessed I hadn't hear about this before. I loved cracker jacks as a kid, but if I had known about M&Ms and popcorn earlier, I probably would have been completely addicted to that stuff and obese.

Ha! Not really. But what tastes good isn't always good for you.

When you check in with your whole being, you start to really work with your value system, whether it's about food or some other aspect of life that's involved. You look at yourself and make decisions based on what's valuable to you. People can have safes at home and deposit boxes in banks to keep the things they value secure, but do they place any value in doing the right thing?

Checking in is the most important safety system that you have. The Earlobes are all about giving you the capacity to evaluate your actions and what is going on in your life. This is the Center where you get to face the habits that work against those values and the ones that work for you positively.

Exercises: Make the Earlobes Center Neutral or Positive

The exercises to make the Earlobes Center neutral are really easy. (This shouldn't to be done when pregnant)

In the first one, you're just going to grab hold of your earlobes and pull down on them. Before you begin, I want you to close your eyes and breathe. As you pull down on your earlobes, watch your breath. Be conscious as you inhale and exhale. This way, it's going to be really hard to be self-deprecating. Breathe deeply to connect to your spirit. So pull powerfully on those earlobes! Pull them down like you mean it and breathe really lovingly and sweetly. Do this for 1-3 minutes.

Another exercise for the Earlobes makes use of the sipping breath method. If you have earrings, take them out first and exhale before you do sipping breathing. Act like you are breathing though a straw and exhale through the nose. You will feel the positive effect immediately. If the Earlobes could only speak, they would surely say: "Oh, my God! That's amazing!" You see, the Sipping Breath technique helps balance your pituitary to secrete more of the hormone Pitocin. There is a point in the earlobes that is associated with your pituitary quite strongly, and it's this point that can be used to switch the pituitary on. An active pituitary brings out your intuition, which counters self-deprecation.

The Moon She Rocks You

If you work your earlobes this way, the score of self-deprecation will be zero and intuition will be 100! You can check out my videos so you can learn how to do Sipping Breath properly.

In the third exercise, take your fingers to the outside of your earlobes; massage all the way up the outside of the ear. Use pressure as you massage them. Breathe and massage while going up and around the outside rim of your ears. I want you to do this exercise three or four times and breathe as you do it. Then massage behind the ears. It helps to release tension. You'll feel the relaxing effect immediately.

Here's another exercise. Think of the movement of the head when you say "yes" and when you say "no." These movements help to release a lot of tension in the neck. Say, "Hu la" while doing this exercise to get your heart involved. The heart is always about connecting, contrary to self-deprecation which is about disconnecting. So, just say, "Huu lllaaaaaaa, huu lllaaaaaaa" for a while as you move the head as if saying yes, then do the same thing as you move the head as if saying no. Do it in each direction for 90 seconds, then inhale, hold your breath, and exhale. You can do this really quickly.

The greatest benefit from all these little exercises is that they also act as interrupters when you find yourself in the negative state of the Earlobes. They interrupt that self-deprecating flow and provide the gift of the Center. The benefit is they help you align to your values and know which should be given importance. Once you get yourself aligned, then you can be of service to yourself and the world. You can be a truly valuable person connected with what you value within yourself. In the Earlobes Center, you will know how incredible you are with your special talents.

The other day I saw these great pictures a friend mine had taken. I walked in and I said, "Oh, my God! These are really great!" They made me think about the times when we start to do something we love and all of a sudden we find out that we are really good at it. That's the wonder of discovering your talent! Making the most of a talent is like a gift that you get to give back to the world, and this increases your value. Remember that being in the Earlobes is the perfect time to do things like plan a family meeting or assess your business. It's also the perfect time to create a mission statement for your life or business and to discover who you really are.

The great thing about a mission statement is that it's made up of just a few words. You don't have to be a great writer to create one! Read mission statements of different businesses and then give yourself time to create your own. Defining a mission statement will help you understand your values. Once you develop the mission statement, stand under those words, not above them. Let them lead the way. Think about it.

Once you get ahold of your values, you can say, "This is the recipe for my life. This is who I am!" I remember telling my mother at the young age of five, that I was going to start my own religious order. I can't say that I have totally done that, but I certainly took the essence of these teachings and done things that other people haven't done. I truly feel it's very important for everyone to be empowered. I want you to be the most valuable person that you can possibly be in this lifetime and on this Earth of ours! The only way you can do that is by unearthing your values. Not all gems are found sitting on the top of the ground! You usually have to dig down to get the really good ones because they are deeply buried.

If you're familiar with a geode, you know it looks like any typical rock, but when you break it open, you expose this entire magical world inside of it. You are like that geode. You need to get inside yourself to see the gems and jewels that are connected to your spirit and to your essence. As you start digging out your gems, you are going to truly understand the things that you value deeply yet unconsciously—the things that you are not willing to do or be without in your life. Kept hidden, you are only like a plain rock in a desert. But expose what's valuable inside of you, and you give back to the world what it has given you from the start.

We are in our Earlobes at the same time each month. Schedule your next family reunion or your next big board meeting when the moon is in your Earlobes so you can talk about the values of your company in a focused and coherent way. Being positive in the Earlobes Moon Center is to know yourself and become yourself.

Empowered in the Earlobes

Being empowered in the Earlobes is all about knowing and acting on your values. Knowing your core values signals the time for connecting with those of like mind and figuring out how to live by your values. If you do not do these things, you will be disempowered.

Disempowered in the Earlobes

Being disempowered in the Earlobes will make you critically over-analyze yourself, your intents, and motives for everything.

Balancing Exercise for the Earlobes

Punching: This involves breaking the inner stranglehold.

Duration: 1-2 minutes

Create an "O" shape with the mouth. Make fists, tucking the thumbs inside your palm. Sit or stand upright and powerfully punch straight in front of you, extending the arms at shoulder level. Rapidly alternate the arms. Allow the body to twist with the motion.

The Gift:

Alleviates frustration and creates new energy. Releases tension in the shoulders and chest. Goodbye frustration! Hello stimulation!

Nape of the Neck

Overview

Are you ready to be really romantic? Are you ready to speak very romantically? When in the Nape of the Neck Moon Center, you *will be* romantic and sexy. Why? It's because you will speak from the heart and be inspired to be around those who can connect heart to heart with you. On the other hand, when you are challenged in this Center, you will feel totally unable to communicate from your heart or even speak in a way that is romantically, truly, and lovingly connected to you partner or anyone else for that matter. You have no desire to communicate with anybody. You feel cold, reserved, and disconnected from the people around you.

The Details

The Nape of the Neck is actually a sexy Moon Center. So what is it about this Center that makes it truly sexy? It's really simple. Many women wear their hair down over their neck, but others wear their hair up. Why? It's because they want it exposed, especially if they have a gorgeous neck. The nape is really very sensitive because it's not exposed all the time, being hidden by the hair. When someone touches it, oh! You feel like your whole body is melting with pleasure. Men will surely love to know about this one. Warning! Women love a romantic, loving, connected voice here. So enter with love and care.

In the positive aspect of the Nape, you are truly romantic and you talk romantically. You may find yourself asking for things that are very romantic to you. You can elicit it by your choice of topics or ask for it. "Darling, would you just tell me something really yummy. I just love the sound of your voice." You want true romance, not necessarily seduction. True romance means you can open yourself up to the infinity—that vastness that is inside of you; to have your soul opened up and romanced. Romancing the soul is what you can do in this Center and you can do that in a million different ways. It's a really yummy center where you are in touch with Divine Romance.

So what happens when you are in the challenged aspect of this Center? Well, you'll feel like saying: "Hey, don't come near me! Don't talk to me!" At this time, you are shut down, shut out, and disconnected from the subtleties of romance. It's because the Nape has so much to do about subtleties, and romance is built on subtleties that may or may not lead to making love. True romance means something else entirely. It's when you can say, "Oh, I know you. I get you and I know what you would really love to have done for you." It's actually all about the beauty of that knowing. The challenge is to counter the feeling of being neither beautiful nor safe that makes you retreat, be cold and protective of yourself.

Romance literally means connecting in a very gracious, almost ceremonial way, with another person. Romance is about another time or space where you take time with everything. It is very patient and beautiful and thoughtful all at the same time. It is the foreplay of life.

Being a romantic means you are beautifully laid out for your partner. It feels so good when you are so deeply connected with someone that you can sense them from a great distance. You can fall in love with someone's voice and hear it even when this wonderful person isn't around. You can use your own voice to be extremely romantic and to connect romantically. This is what I fell in love with first with my partner. I could fall into the palm of God on the strains of his voice. I once told him he could recite the ABCs to me and I would drink it all in.

Think of all the singers we know as crooners. They romanced the heart, or at least the body. With a heavenly romantic voice, you can invite someone to connect to you, romance their soul, and even sway the heavens! This is what you can do when the Moon's energy is in your Nape of the Neck.

You can use your voice to create vibrations that resonate out the back of your neck. To feel the vibration, put your hand on the back of your neck and speak. You will feel the sound box vibrating. When you sing and chant, it vibrates even more as air passes through the throat. Your vocal cords get played like a guitar. This is your magical tool!

We were walking down the promenade one night in Santa Monica and there was this little girl who was 5 feet tall and probably weighed only 85 pounds. Amazingly, she had a voice that was as big as the sky, but it was raspy. I knew it was dehydrated because she was not getting enough fluids. This was causing her vocal cords to dry up. She really had no connection with the romantic because her juiciness was dry. We are like that at times.

When you are unable to feel that romantic connection, you are going to experience ineffective communication. You'll think nobody listens to you or pays attention to you when you talk. You feel that you aren't connecting with anyone. Unable to connect, you start fights and disconnect from those close to you, even when you could do something to have a more heart-centered communication. To fix this, you need to experience that you have the ability to uplift yourself through your vibration, your means of communication. You can pray, you can sing, you can chant. I love the verses that are about Suni-ai. Suni-ia means "to listen with every fiber of your being." There are four verses in Jap Ji (this beautiful prayer of Guru Nanak's that he wrote upon being liberated) explaining the bliss of "listening" with every part of your being. Uttered, these words will help you to open yourself to the romance present in someone else's voice, to listen to and receive it. Listening is the key to get out of the feeling of being unheard.

Recipe: Juice Mixes for Throat Issues

Now, let's talk about food in relation to the Nape of the Neck. To be conscious of your food intake can help achieve the positive and neutral aspects of this Center. But it's not all about eating. When your throat is really closed down for instance, the last thing you want to think about is eating. In that case, drink a beverage that is warm or is at room temperature, like lime water, lemon water, or a comforting tea. There are lots of wonderful things you can drink. Pineapple juice is really good for throat issues. Ginger tea and Throat comfort tea are favorites of mine. When I feel my throat is getting a little weird, I just mix fresh lemon juice and ginger in my blender and then strain the pulp out afterwards. After taking a shot of it, I say, "Oh, my God, such relief!" It's also great for your immune system. You can do the same thing with crushed pineapple and fresh ginger to make a throat-relieving drink. It's a great tonic! These homemade preparations are really relaxing to the throat and will help you to feel and be attuned to the vibratory frequency of your capacity to commune. Pineapple juice is a godsend to singers.

Recipe: Gargle Mix to Open Up the Throat

I suppose you already know that when your throat feels really closed down and constricted, you should gargle with warm salt water. If you put in a little pinch of turmeric in there, it will work a lot better. Turmeric is so great for so many things. It's best for the mucous membranes that protect your throat, which has more mucous membrane area than any other part of the body. Also a spray called Saving Grace for singers is a great on-the-spot spray.

But no matter how much turmeric or ginger you use, a salt gargle is not going to give you the capacity to open up the Nape of the Neck and the chakra associated with it. In this case, what you need to do is wear beautiful jewelry! Just wear any stone that is blue and beautiful!

Lapis lazuli is for giving fearlessness. Turquoise is for healing. You can get those that are blue and those with a hue that moves towards green, such as fluorite, which has a color that borders on blue. Also, blue topaz and aquamarine are great.

Such blue stones are really good for the throat. Wear them regularly and they will provide you with constant aid. You will gain the capacity to speak better, to be heard, and to be unafraid of delivering your message and expressing your thoughts. These will work whether you're a public speaker or someone who just needs to say something.

Mantras: Open Up the Nape Center

Whatever stone you use, you must remember that it's never a good time to give a speech when in the challenged aspect of the Nape. Fortunately, you can open up this Center quickly by chanting "Wah wah hey hey wah wah hey hey wah wah hey hey guru." If you do some chanting every day, you will feel so much better. Wah means wow! But it's not like the ordinary wow—it's the infinite, vast kind of wow! Guru, on the other hand, means the remover of darkness or the one who takes you out of the darkness and into the light. You can listen to these chants on the DVDs of the program.

There is really almost no breath in between the words when you say them. Do this chant for a couple of minutes in a very staccato fashion; this breaks fear. In this time, you will experience how it opens up and relaxes your jaw, which is the conduit for your voice. Once your jaw is relaxed, your vocal cords also start relaxing and you will feel more openness in the nape of the neck. This chant is very romantic because you are connecting with that flow of the infinite. Saying wah wah recreates that beautiful flow which is like water as it settles down serenely on the earth. You must speak this chant like you are taking a pledge. You should feel it right on either side of your neck.

To do this chant properly, inhale deeply and close your eyes. Listen to the sound that you create yourself. First breathe in and out, and then say, "Wah wah hey hey wah wah hey hey wah wah hey hey guru, wah wah hey hey wah wah hey hey wah wah hey hey guru, wah wah hey hey wah wah hey hey wah wah hey hey guru, wah wah hey hey wah wah hey hey wah wah hey hey guru, wah wah hey hey wah wah hey hey wah wah hey hey guru, wah wah hey hey wah wah hey hey wah wah hey hey guru." Inhale and press the tongue to the roof of the mouth and pull your chin back and exhale. The more that you do this chant, the faster you will click into it. You will feel it makes you bright, open, and ready to invite other people in because that's really what communication is all about. It's about common union and that's what you are looking for here.

Now here's another chant that you can also do on your own. It goes like this, "Wahe Guru Wahe Guru Wahe Wahe Wahe Guru," Wahe Guru Wahe Guru Wahe Wahe Wahe Guru," Then you whisper: "Sa Ta Na Ma." If you recall, Sa Ta Na Ma means life, birth, death, and rebirth. Sat Nam means: "Truth is my identity." To do this exercise, you need to close your eyes before you chant. You will discover this sound can really vibrate within you.

This is the vibration of ecstasy, which can readjust you to get your communication with the world back and bring that identity of truth back into you, allowing you to be that truth. You must do the chant at least six times but 11 to 22 minutes work best. "Wahe Guru Wahe Guru Wahe Wahe Wahe Guru Wahe Guru Wahe Guru Wahe Wahe Wahe Guru Sa Ta Na Ma." After you have completed the last one, inhale, hold the sound and exhale, and place your hands over your heart.

The self-care aspect of the Nape of the Neck is realized by asking a few questions.

- Do you feel you are communing with yourself powerfully?
- Do you love your voice?
- Do you feel you have the capacity to receive?
- Do you believe you can be compassionate with others and with yourself?

- Do you experience that you can hear and fall in love with an unfamiliar voice?

The truth is that you can fall in love with your voice and you can fall in love with that voice of the infinite that comes through you because you yourself are that voice of God. Yes, you! Sing, chant, and create the vastness! Do things for yourself that relaxes you so that you can feel compassionate, not uptight. Have you ever met somebody who is both uptight and compassionate? I don't think so! They simply don't co-mingle. You are either one or the other. So knowing this, you must remember to do something for yourself that allows you to have the space to communicate with yourself. Take a bath. Go to the spa. These quiet and relaxing activities will do the job.

There's already so much noise in our life that blocks communication, and we add to the din by switching on gadgets like the TV, the iPod and other electronic noisemakers wherever we are. We have all these things making noise simultaneously and so we can't hear ourselves think! There always seems to be an email to be answered or a call to be taken. There is always something to distract us. What you need is time to attract, and to attract yourself first. If you don't take the time to commune with your own being by creating your own sacred silence, you lose the ability to be sensitive to what others are trying to say to you. You also lose the ability to hear or trust your own intuition.

My daughter is in med school and facing this incredible challenge to her health at the same time. She has to balance her time between studying, getting enough sleep and meditating to try to change the frequency of what is going on with her. This effort makes all the difference in this troubled society of ours that keeps us off balance and unaware. So don't wait until you get some huge disease before you get a realization or epiphany to establish communication with the Infinite. In order to realize how deeply important you are in life in spite of all the distractions around you, create sacred spaces for yourself where you will hear what's truly important coming from the spirit. It's called "Allowing the Divine to Romance You."

"I don't even know what to say!" somebody said to me one day when I shared what was happening with my daughter. I replied, "That is the most truthful response there is, because there really is nothing to say. There is only the way to pray, meditate, and be one with that communion of light." Although sometimes there isn't anything to be said, if we always feel we don't know what to say, it means we have lost our ability to commune with ourselves. Our old concept of romance aside, communion is not just between us and someone else. It's really connecting with our whole being, but this is only the starting place.

To be able to commune, you need to listen first. These ears of ours are the listeners, the Suni-ai, which are always deeply listening. But they are not the only ones with the sense of hearing. The heart is another listening device. Listen with these tools when it's all quiet. In the stillness, you create lusciousness and vastness; you can hear beyond the sounds around you and your response is appropriate, adequate, and truly romantic.

When you think of romance, you don't think of romancing up against a wall. If romance is what you're after, you go to a beautiful place, like the beach, the woods, a favorite restaurant, or the vacation hotel near *that* lake. There is always a voluptuousness or vastness to a place of romance which is so unlike the sensation felt in a dingy little motel room where you often end up unplanned. Romance is about beauty and connection. Creating romance in your everyday life will help to balance the Nape center.

Exercises: Promote Flow of Energy in the Nape

Sometimes, just a handful of words is so much better than a lot of words. Chant, meditate, sing, and do the things that allow freedom of the Nape of the Neck. Tap it! Did you know that by just tapping on the back of your neck, you can release some of the tension which holds up this heavy thing we call our head? Your neck is a conduit and it holds up that melon, that is our head!

The neck is just like a trunk line from our body to our melon. It's where energy from all of the lower parts of our body moves up to the brain, which vibrates with a frequency that shines like light! Thus we are called *Hueman* beings—a light of the mind. The Nape of the Neck is the 3rd eye of your astral body. This center is super intuitive.

One little thing that you can do to promote the flow of energy through the neck is to raise your hands, interlace your fingers and place them on your nape. Now push up against your occipital ridge, and open your elbows really wide, effectively activating your heart. Do this with an "O" breath.

Make an "O" of your mouth and inhale and exhale through this opening. You can also do this with a quick continuous breath called "O" Breath—Breath of Fire. This will give you energy. The regular "O" Breath will calm you.

Empowered in the Nape of the Neck

To be empowered in the Nape is to be romantic. It's the time when you must pay attention to what or who you are attracting if you're not in a committed relationship. It's when you feel and speak from the heart but it's also when you must watch yourself carefully in order to keep from diving headfirst into relationships that seem yummy and romantic in the moment. When your Moon Center changes position, you will wonder what you were thinking back then and why you ever made such a mistake. Be open-hearted and open-voiced. An open-intuition can help you steer away from falling for anyone who speaks in a romantic way to you before you test the reality of their intentions.

Disempowered in the Nape of the Neck

This is the time when you will find it hard to connect and may even be unwilling to communicate.

Balancing Exercise for the Nape of the Neck

Meridian Face Massage: In this exercise, you say, "Spa-aahh."

Duration: 1-2 minutes

Tap your temples, the back of your neck, the shoulders, and the chest, then, tap the top of your head and the TMJ points (located in front of the ears on the connective jaw point). Lastly, brush over the third eye point (center of the brow) in an upward motion.

The Gift:

This is a great and easy pressure releaser; a rejuvenator. So, indulge!

Nipples

Overview

Everyone would want to be around you when the moon is in the Nipples Moon Center. Here, you are overly compassionate and giving. There is just not enough that you can do for everyone! When you are neutral here, you radiate with unconditional love. You are "there" with everyone. Unbalanced, it's Victim City! You enter "woe is me" central where compassion turns bad.

The Details

After the Nape of the Neck come the Nipples. Remember, this is in the chart but this may not hold true for you. Your nipples may or may not follow your nape. You'll get this later on. So what makes the Nipples special? Well, it's that fabulous arch line in women that goes from nipple to nipple over your heart.

Men don't have this arch, just you women. When in the positive state, you are over giving—like Mother Teresa on steroids!

116

You are like: "Oh, I can do this and that for you." You can easily get exhausted while taking care of everyone. In the neutral aspect, you are also extremely compassionate and present; you will not get over extended. You are not looking for validation in the neutral. You simply show a precise and concise compassion. In the challenged aspect of this Center, you feel incredibly insecure about your gifts and you act closed, unfeeling, and hard-hearted, as if you have nothing to give. (This often shows up when exhausted)

The Nipple is where the arch line originates and ends. When your energy is in the Nipples, you tend to want to give and serve by volunteering your time and expertise. If you are taking care of a parent, you feel you can do more. If you feel like giving love to someone you simply can't do enough. Realize that help doesn't have to be physical on the earth. There's the power of prayer, meditation and more subtle levels of support. Allow yourself to know instinctively whom to help.

This Moon Center is where your life becomes more effortless, not more effortful. When you are in this over giving state, you know that everybody around you is going to love being with you. Who wouldn't want to do that when they know you are going to want to cook for them, do all their laundry, and maybe even give them a massage. Charting with the help of The Moon She Rocks You program will give you the capacity to plan ahead and to utilize the gift you receive properly. When you are over giving in the positive state, you are going to come home at the end of the day exhausted.

When you are in the neutral state and feeling compassionate, you allow this Center's energy to flow through. I have had so many people tell me, "You are a mother with a sick child. It must feel so bad!" I just say, "That's not what this is about. This is about a journey into healing."

When you are in the compassionate state, it's very different because you are neutral. You see what needs to be done and you know you can do it. When you are sympathetic, you are bleeding from your heart. When you are empathetic, you'd likely say: "Oh, my God, they are having such a hard time I really feel their pain." Empathy means that you feel for somebody, while sympathy means that you feel with whoever is in need. Either feeling isn't beneficial for you or the person at the receiving end, because there is a kind of cloying energy to them.

My daughter isn't talking to anybody at this point in time because she doesn't want sympathy. She doesn't want to hear the stories people want to tell her. I too have stopped calling people who want to share their stories with me because I need to stay neutral and compassionate so that I can be the prayer and meditation conduit for my daughter.

When you are in the Nipples, you get really tuned in to compassion. One day I heard that the Dalai Lama meditates two hours a day on compassion. When I advise people to meditate for 11 minutes, they usually say, "I don't think I can!" Really? The Dalai Lama can find two hours a day to meditate on compassion, but the average people can't fit eleven minutes for that in their schedule? The Dalai Lama saw how his country, Tibet, was invaded and his people slaughtered. Now his land is totally occupied by China and he lives in exile. Tibet will never go back to how it was as we know it, but somehow, by keeping compassion alive, that underlying connection among the Buddhist, the prayerful, meditative psyche is coming back to the Tibetan people. You too can be part of this. Meditate. Chant. Pray each day.

When we women are in the positive state of the Nipples, we can feed the entire world through our compassionate nature, but if we are feeling stuck and miserly, we start to say things that only get us even more stuck in the rut we're in, like, "I don't have enough money" or "I can't do this because I don't have enough to go by!" Reality-check! It will always be not enough if we don't do something to stop feeling closed down!

In my yoga classes, I see how students find it hard to do all the exercises that open up the heart and put pressure on the nipples. It's hard because these exercises lead them to a vulnerable and venerable place inside of themselves, leaving them exposed. To the uninitiated, it can be scary. When we women have our heart closed, we become really critical of everybody and everything. There is almost zero patience and nothing seems right.

The result is that we usually have to go and clean up the mess we've made by saying things like: "I apologize" or "I am sorry I said that you. I wasn't in my right mind."

My favorite hairdresser uses only natural ingredients. There is no horrible smell in her salon. You can get your haircut, oil treatment, hair coloring, you name it, and you won't get sick from any chemical smells. She did an oil treatment on me once and I loved her so much I probably sent 10 people to her who became clients. One of them told me, "I went there and I went crazy because I did not like the color she used on my hair. I don't think she will see me again. I was so PMSed I called and told her I hated my color." I suggested she call her back to explain and to apologize. Remove the drama from the trauma. Use your heart to bail yourself out.

If you have had a similar outburst and you are sorry for saying all the things you did, please don't use the PMS card! We can always tell people we are PMSing, but the truth is there is just one thing we could say, "I was only having a completely disconnected, impatient, heartless day and I am so sorry I did not accept your gift." Then you could say what you would like to see done differently in any situation.

People can lose their heart temporarily. To get it back, you just need to know how to breathe properly. When you really breathe powerfully, your lungs massage your heart. The heart always yearns for the massage the lungs can provide. Who doesn't want to get a good massage? Most people love having a massage as it helps to release the tension that shuts down the body and turns it into something similar to a door with rusty hinges. When tension bogs us down, we become like a squeaky door! To fix this, we must do exercises, like that open up the heart.

For a quick yoga fix, you can interlace your fingers into a Venus lock or the lock of love (all the fingers are interlaced with each other) and place it in front of your 3rd eye area without touching it. Breathe 90 seconds to 3 minutes. This will adjust the frontal lobe of your brain which rules your personality. This can calm your personality down and allow your intuition to rule.

Exercises: Especially for the Heart

There are so many exercises for the heart. Here, you'll learn the most important ones. The first exercise is about wisdom. The version I am about to teach you will stimulate your heart. You will use "O" breath which engages the vagus nerve through the meridian that goes through the center of the lips. The vagus nerve connects the heart to the mind. Your fingers are to be interlaced in the Venus lock. From the nipples, you are going to bring your hands down really powerfully on the exhale and back up to the nipple level on the inhale. All breathing through "O" breath (mouth in an O). You will feel the effect 30 seconds into the exercise, but you won't stop there. You will do it for 3 minutes. Now, I know you're probably thinking: "Oh, my God, three minutes? Are you serious?" Yes, even longer.

This is another very simple one. Are you ready? Close your eyes. Visualize looking at your third eye—a great focus point. Bring your arms up to create a 60 degree angle and it will be shaped like a V. Your heart will be in the center of the V. This is a path to channel energy right into your heart. Inhale, stretch the arms up at the 60 degree angle and exhale. Bring your hands over your heart, left under and right over. Try it for 3 minutes or longer.

I'm sure you are quite familiar with the saying: "Your ego is a great servant but a bad master." Why is this so? Simply put, when your ego is in charge, your life is hell. It's just not fun. But when your ego serves your spirit, it's really fabulous. Your life may not be any "better," but your perspective can be. Sadly, in this material world of ours, our ego is set by default to serve the body and not the spirit. Yet, only the spirit can bring mental and emotional peace.

Exercise: For Managing the Ego

The next exercise is to manage the ego. It is really simple to do and clears the heart of all the debris of the past. Sit up and create fists with your hands. Rotate them away from your heart, doing the "O" breath again. Do this as fast as you can for 3 minutes. The nipples play a big role here because they protect the heart. By clearing the heart, you will feel connected again. You'll also feel that you belong and that you can be compassionate with yourself and others. This is really a good thing to do when you just need to release the situation that's keeping you in a disconnected state. While doing it think: "I am, I am."

You have 72,000 nerve endings in your hands and you get to play with them and to stimulate them all. Isn't that fabulous? Doesn't it feel great when you activate all the parts of your hands powerfully? By stimulating their nerve points, you clear the connection with your heart and allow your nipples to protect it. Think about your nipples now. Don't you love having them sucked when someone makes love to you, or when you nurse your child? They are very powerful, aren't they? They make you feel really deeply.

I'm sure you can feel energy in your hands sometimes. When you feel pain in your body or emotionally challenged in one of your Moon Centers, place your hands there, and you will feel the healing energy flow. Did you know that if you do the motion of dusting your hands for a minute, you actually charge and energize them? You can use this energy anywhere you want.

Exercises: To Connect with the Heart (2-3 min.)

The following exercise is very simple. Put your hands over your beautiful nipples. In this position, you are going to twist side to side as far as you can. Inhale to your left, let your head move with your body, and exhale to your right. Inhale deeply and exhale. Good, right?

This one is going to be difficult because you need to put your hands in a Venus Lock. Do it by pressing your thumbs together behind your back, and then you bow while chanting, "Ong So Hung Ong So Hung." Inhale as you come up from your bow. Ong means "the Creator in the process of creation" and So Hung means "I am thou." This supports true connection and stimulates the heart center in the back. You are bowing to your essence.

The vibration of certain sounds can totally adjust a Moon Center like the Nipples. Hum is one of those sounds, which is a Heart Center sound. It works effectively to vibrate the heart area. You just say, "Hum, hum,

hum." It's simple enough. Inhale before you start, then exhale while chanting hum.

Hummmmmmmmmmmmmmm...
Hummmmmmmmmmmmmmmm ...
Hummmmmmmmmmmmmmmm...

Do five to 500 hums and get rid of negative energy. You can chant behind the wheel when driving, just don't close your eyes. Inhale and hold this sound, then exhale to end.

This exercise totally recalibrates you. It creates synchronization with all the parts of you. You come together at your heart and your nipples.

Use this sound resonance every day for at least 11 minutes. This way, you will not get yourself stuck in the challenged aspect of the Nipples because you will generate this radiant vibration that will offset any negativity in and around you. Do it! Experience it and bring forth your real compassion.

Empowered in the Nipples

You are Mother Teresa on steroids. You are compassionate to everyone, including yourself. You see what needs to be done and do it. You are vast in your connection to all.

Disempowered in the Nipples

Here, you are a close-hearted and a self-absorbed victim. You get the urge to eat really unnecessary and bad things for your body which makes you feel worse. A sugar binge takes precedence, but that only leaves a bad taste as it doesn't empower you.

Balancing Exercise for the Nipples

Heart Clearing: This exercise works to "get it off your chest."

Duration: 1-2 minutes

With firm hands and your fingers stiff, make a chopping motion in front of your body, go down from the shoulders to the waist at a 60-degree angle, cutting a "V" around the heart. Put emphasis on the downward motion. Do this sitting or standing. For added benefit, make a simple "O" shape of your mouth and inhale/exhale quickly as you move the hands up and down quickly.

The Gift:

This is an instant stress reducer and helps release tension and thoughts that are creating pressure on your heart.

Navel

Overview

In the Navel, you will have lots of very powerful energy. Directed and creative, you are on top of and empowered in the world. Your physical energy is great and your stamina is good. Unbalanced, you feel weak and unstable, like the earth is moving under your feet and you experience the proverbial "rug-is-being-pulled-out-from-under-you" feeling.

The Details

The navel is also commonly known as the bellybutton—we all know that one. But what is the Navel Moon Center about? Well, this is all about strength, power, and energy. These are its positive aspects, which are fabulous! The challenged aspect of this, of course, is not so fabulous, because it's when you feel really unstable, unsure, and undecided on a lot of things, and it's like, "Um, should I start with this or not?" You want somebody to tell you want to do and how to do it. Without advice, you can't act. When you're in the neutral aspect of this Center, you realize how you can use your energy in a very stable and calm way—you don't just dump energy out all at once or throw your energy away.

The Navel is the place of energy in the body. It started out as the feeding tube which connected you to your mother's feeding station. It's now that area which you use to feed your energy to the world. In this Center, you know that you are energy. Working in the positive of the Navel, you are aware of energy and know how to get it. You know how to uplift yourself and others in more ways than one.

When you are challenged in this Center, you have no energy and you feel tired. It's like you can't do anything because your projection in the world is null. You think you are so little! "What difference can I make?" you might ask yourself. Fortunately, there's always a remedy when challenged.

I love that story about kids between 8 and 11 years old who decided to go out and collect pennies to build schools for children in Afghanistan and Pakistan. Children can do amazing things! They have this kind of mindset that just kicks in when they decide that something needs to be done. With the energy they have, they just go and make things happen. It's that simple to them.

As adults, we need to convince ourselves to be fearless. With the use of the Navel Center, we can do that easily! It's only about how you get energy and where you get it from. If you love something, you are going to get energy from it. So think of the things in your life that you love. Think about situations that you love. You can write down as many as you want. It can be visiting friends, dancing, singing, or playing a musical instrument, and all the people you love. Whatever it is that you love, write it down in a list so you don't forget what gives you real energy.

Exercise is really important because exercise moves your energy. In Kundalini yoga, we have lots of exercises for the Navel that make you feel empowered and strong. The first thing you must do when you feel stuck and without energy is to move. Dance, run, swim, get on a gym machine and do rowing exercises. Some people say we need to do 20 minutes of aerobic exercise every day to stay healthy. What I say is: "If you ever want to change your state of mind, you must get up and move!"

Things just don't happen by sitting on a therapist's couch, and while we all need mentors, helping ourselves through exercise is truly necessary. That's what yoga is about! Through yoga, you can access your energy to create the consciousness of being united within, which is what really matters. Do you know the saying "United we stand, divided we fall"? That applies here.

Exercise: Breath of Fire

When you feel utterly divided and disconnected from your energy source, you don't know how to uplift yourself and you can't uplift others. There is an unlimited amount of energy out there, and you can make it yours using Breath of Fire. This is such a priceless way for getting energy and we are going to use it in two different ways.

The easiest way to learn Breath of Fire is to lie down on your back, stretch your arms up over your head and just allow your diaphragm to be really loose. You will do it slowly at first and then gradually build up your pace to very quick.

This breath is a continuous and rapid diaphragmatic breath. Here you want the diaphragm to extend upward when you inhale and collapse when you exhale. Close your eyes and just feel it. You have to experience it from inside of you. Keep your eyes closed while doing the breath through your nose. Continue inhaling and exhaling rapidly without stopping the breath. If you start feeling a little spacey and hyperventilated, you can pull up on the rectum and sex organ. The action will ground you.

Once you have learned Breath of Fire, you'll be able to do it anywhere and anytime, except after the 4th month of pregnancy, the first 3 days of your menstrual cycle, and when you want to go to sleep. What are great times to use Breath of Fire? Whenever you need energy! You can even do it while taking a shower in the morning (except when you are doing the cold part of your shower) or brushing your hair in front of the mirror. This is going to be your new energy source. Forget energy products like Full Throttle, Red Bull, and the like. I am telling you, Breath of Fire is the bomb! Just allow yourself some time to become familiar with it and don't get frustrated. It's true that learning it is often a little challenging because so many of us reverse breath, but the more you do this breathing, the more you will experience how really fabulous and energizing it is.

This is the Energy Gurus Energy Breath - http://youtu.be/2HekygUdi94 shown here.

Exercise: Clearing and Connecting Done on an Empty Stomach.

Here's another exercise that really clears you out and makes you feel connected again. You are going to sit on your heels. You can place a pillow between your buttocks and your feet if needed. You can also put padding under your feet. Press your fists on either side of your navel. Exhale really powerfully through the mouth as you bend forward as far as you can. Keep pressing your hands deeply on either side of your navel and massage the area very powerfully. Keep the breath out as you continue the massage. Inhale as you come up to a sitting position. Do this three more times. This is very powerful and should not be done while pregnant or on the first 3 days of your menstrual cycle.

Exercise: Energizing the Navel

Now let's talk about energizing the Navel. To do this, you need to feel your aortic pulse in the navel. Here's the exercise that will do the trick. You are going to lie down on your back and stick one or two fingers in your navel, not your thumb, it has a pulse of it's own. Feel inside the middle of your navel. It's going to feel a little weird at first, but I want you to feel its pulse. If the pulse is not right in the middle, try to feel around the immediate outside area to locate the pulse. If you want to set this pulse so it is in the middle of your navel (which means it is set properly to your aortic connection), then do this exercise.

Inhale lying on your back and go to a sitting position. Exhale back down to a prone position. Do this 11 times.

The area around the navel affects your digestion. You get constipated or get diarrhea if this aortic pulse is off. In women, this puts a lot of pressure on your female organs and effects your hormones. By doing either of these exercises you can reset this pulse so it serves you as it is meant to.

Now I have already mentioned energy drinks. They are very popular and contain lots of caffeine but I call them fake energizers because they drain your adrenals and weaken your body. Instead of resorting to caffeine drinks, think of things in your life that truly energize you. These are the things you love doing. Hold them dear to you because they will recharge you. Have you ever noticed that when you feel energized, life becomes so much easier? When you feel drained, everything seems harder and hurts. Feeling energized depends also on eating the right foods. People often pick the wrong foods for energy. Knowing about energy foods is a good start.

The beauty of yoga is that it recharges you and works on different aspects of your being. There are so many yoga exercises for the Navel Center. I can't explain them all here, but I assure you that they are priceless! I suggest you learn more of these exercises in The Moon She Rocks You video series and start experiencing the many benefits from doing them. (http://gurutej.com/store/11-moon-centers)

Here's a story. One day, I was talking to this woman I was teaching. She said that she was from a specific country and that she loved the food from that country. She also confided that she had to take a lot of laxative. I recommended some colonics for her, and asked about the food from her country that she loved. Hmm, no veggies, and she ate nothing with much fiber. I suggested changing her eating habits. I asked her if she liked salad, and she declared, "I hate salads."

I realized then that she wanted to get better without changing her diet, which was the cause of her problem. What she really needed was to make salads her new best friends. Salads have lots of greens and roughage that can go through and clean out your intestinal tract. After eating a salad, you get a whole lot of energy. All it takes to be in good health is knowledge and acceptance.

A lot of people have told me how they just get a whole frozen cake, or pie or a quart of ice cream, sit down in front of the TV, and eat. Comforting and filling, yes, but these foods only steal energy from the body. To prevent energy loss, we must eat a lot of raw green food and a lot of alkaline food such as quinoa, millet, amaranth, and brown rice. These are great grains with magical powers of rejuvenation. Every food has a gift of energy. The yellow veggies have plenty of antioxidants and the greens, calcium and minerals; reds and violets are usually great for the blood and liver. Knowing the gift of the food you eat is a really wonderful thing. You can start teaching your kids about energy foods and where they come from.

Have you ever cleaned out your closet? It feels so good, right? You look at it, see it orderly and clean, and you tell yourself, "I got space!" and you feel so relieved. It's the same thing when your body gets cleansed by eating energizing greens. All of a sudden, you realize that you have more energy and more discernment on how to use your energy. The beauty of the neutral mind in the Navel is that you don't just go and say: "I got energy and I am throwing and splashing it all over the place!" Instead, you take care of the energy you have gained lovingly and calmly. Think of your energy as a precious pearl. The foods that give you energy are equally important and valuable, so know what these are.

We all have the nature of an angel and a beast. Who's in charge is just a matter of which one you feed. When you feed yourself junk, you are feeding the beast, and it has little patience. Women act like that sometimes. The beauty of this Center is that it allows you be the grace under pressure, the power and the essence of who you really are. It makes you feel full of energy, alive, and capable of sustaining and supporting what is around you. We were molded to be energetic beings. We have been given the ability to get energy, to see it, and to be that energy.

How hard is it to get anything done when you don't have energy? It's really, really hard! I don't want your life to be hard. I want you to have energy! Decide how best to use this energy to do what is needed in your life now. I want you to remember Breath of Fire. I want you to remember how to bow forward knowing that in that simple action, you can simultaneously clear your head and get your digestion working properly. I want you to know that there are so many ways of getting energy from your food and from what you drink. This is really how you get your life going.

Empowered in the Navel

You are the power source. You are in touch with your energy. When really balanced in the Navel, you will deliver on your word and you will empower others. Channel and use this energy wisely and for the good of all.

Disempowered in the Navel

You feel vulnerable, exposed, and crazy to an extent. In this state, it will help if you go to a group yoga class for meditation. You will need a friend to take with you. This should be someone who is willing to give a part of his or her energy to you to get you motivated. Being disempowered, you won't see this is necessary or want anything to do with anyone, and yet, you need to trust someone. Only a person who isn't blind can lead the blind, and in the disempowered state, you are blind, so get some help.

Balancing Exercise for the Navel

Insanity Breath: Contrary to how it's named, this exercise is really a calm and clarity booster.

Duration: 3 minutes (mouth wide open the entire time)

Place the tip of the tongue to the roof of the mouth. Open the mouth as wide as possible. Keep it open the entire time. Breathe long and deep through the nose. When finished, shake the head while keeping the mouth loose and relaxed. This sounds so easy, but you will want to relax your mouth. Be vigilant.

The Gift:

This breaks up "insane" thought patterns, allowing you to see a stressful situation more clearly. Helps balance the adrenal glands and give you the calm to cope.

Inner Thighs

Overview

When you are in the Inner Thighs Moon Center, you feel very connected and solid in your knowingness. Nothing will move you and you are sure of yourself. You are stable in your thoughts and have great creative strength. You will conform to nothing unless it makes sense to you and empowers you. On the other hand, its downside or the weak state is often characterized by sheer disorganization and disconnectedness. In this state, you generally experience difficulty in being creative, you have difficulty in making things happen, and spontaneity is absent.

The Details

Have you ever thought about your inner thighs? Well, they are amazingly delicate areas of your body but are also quite strong body parts. A large number of nerves pass through them. The nerve plexus runs from the digestive system all the way down to the knees. This network passes through the inner thighs, which is why they are truly very nervy areas. Yogi Bhajan used to call them sex nerves, but they all have their own names. If you're interested in their technical names please google online.

Most people have no connection with their inner thighs. When I am teaching yoga, I say, "Okay, squeeze your inner thighs so that you can actually lift up on the root lock, or the area of the genitals and rectum," but most people don't know how to squeeze their thighs. What does that mean? It means they need to connect with their solid, confirmative power—the power that allows them to become structured enough to know exactly what to do, when and how.

In the positive aspect of the Inner Thighs Moon Center, you're easily able to say, "I am consolidated, confirmed, and can conform to this confirmation." The energy is structured and powerful, although not in the same way as in the Navel Center, which is more physical. In the Inner Thighs, you need to create energy that will allow you to feel more connected and consolidated in your total being.

144

When the Inner Thighs Center is in the challenged aspect, you will be disorganized and indecisive. The real challenge here is overcoming indecision. "Should I clear out this drawer or watch a movie? Should I clean this mess of a desk or just leave it alone?" It just feels like nothing is organized.

The neutral aspect of this Center is characterized by a feeling of a tremendous amount of creative strength. You have the foundation already in place, you have control and confirmation, and you can expand your being from that foundation. You can be very creative and feel very alive!

The Inner Thigh Moon Center is about organization or the lack of it in the challenged aspect. Its neutral aspect is creative strength. To get the best of this Moon Center, you need grounding.

The act of squeezing your inner thighs gets you grounded. When you squeeze them, you instantly create great internal organization and strength. Just try it right now. It does not matter whether you're sitting or standing. If you are standing, have your feet a hip width apart and make sure the heels are aligned behind the toes. Most people stand with their toes out, which locks the pelvis and doesn't allow you to effectively squeeze the inner thighs. This is especially applies to women with their wider hips.

Exercise: To Improve Sex Life

You can put a pillow between your inner thighs and practice squeezing against it so that you can feel both the pillow and the energy from your root lock. You can also lie down on your back and do leg lifts with a pillow between your legs and don't let it drop.

When you are in peri-menopause, tissue and muscles start descending from your face and everywhere else. You develop saddlebags and your inner thighs get saggy. Luckily for us, the thigh squeezing exercise can take care of this problem. It is an exercise that you can do anytime and anywhere, as it is barely noticeable. Just squeeze the thighs towards each other. The squeezing and releasing will make you sit up straighter and also lift the rectum and sex organ. This will improve your sex life immensely and give you the strength to become organized and to consolidate your energy. It is a great combo.

When you are in the positive aspect of the Inner Thighs, you feel like you can organize the entire universe. In this state, it's the perfect time to clean up the office or your house; to organize a simple thing as a closet or something more complex, like a group of people, and some do team-building stuff. You will understand how to pull things together into a workable situation and be able to see how the pieces fall together. It's also a great time to meditate on anything in your life as you are not blocked by thoughts that interfere with your inner sight.

If things feel like they are coming apart, meditate. In time, you will see the connective cords of organization and you'll instantly know how to pull them together.

When you think of organizations, you think of them being structured systematically, and yet you know everybody has their own unique way to organize things. Everybody has the gift to see that something could flow better if organized differently. Let's say, for instance, that you want something to put your eyeglasses into before going to bed but don't want it to be a hard case; you just want to put them into something that will keep them safe, not scratch them, and be easy to remove. Now, that "something" might not be there yet, but you can create it, for sure. You can pull things together!

Pulling something together can be done in a million ways: to create a new product, a new way to run your household, a way to de-clutter your office, or an easier way to train your dog. You pull things together as you create new patterns in your life so you don't do the same old ineffective things you used to do. You need to create a new pattern to leave the old ones behind.

If you want to stop doing something in your life, such as smoking, you must make the act of changing more powerful than the unwanted habit. That's what organization is about. I usually tell people, "Your altar should be so beautiful that you actually want to sit down in front of it and meditate." In the same way, you should organize your life with you at its center. Organize it to include your passions and to draw you towards what you really desire. Don't say, "I have always done it like this; it's the only way I know how to do it." To people who think this way, I can only say, "Get over it or expect more of the same."

Exercises: Taking the Inner Thighs to the Positive State

Here are exercises to help you reach the positive state of the Inner Thighs. Through them, you will know each aspect of this Center and what it has in store for you in detail.

This exercise is really good and easy to do. While you do it, you say the mantras "Hu" and "La". Inhale through your mouth saying "Huuuuuuuuuuu" and open your eyes wide at the same time. Exhale through the mouth saying "Laaaaaaaaaaa" and close your eyes at the same time. Hu La is a heart-centered sound. With "Huuuuuuuuuuuuuu," you suck in the entire Universe and as you exhale and say, "Laaaaaaaaaaa," you share your song with the world and bless it.

Stand up and make your hands into claws. Inhale and stand on your toes. At the same time, sweep your arms up from your sides and make claws with your hands and have them face each other above your head. Open your eyes wide and inhale by saying "Huuuuuuuuuuuuu." Now, squat down, landing on your heels, and swing your arms down. Close your eyes and say "Laaaaaaaaaa." Continue for 3 minutes.

You can do this exercise along with me on YouTube. This is the link to the special video of The Energy Guru Claw Dance – http://youtu.be/gmoOXL7MjIY.

Let's do it one more time. Now press your palms together with power and inhale. Take that breath in and hold it. Press at your heart and then exhale.

Exercise: Send Vibrations Down Your Body

Here is another exercise that sends vibrations down your whole body. Here you say, "Har Har Har Har Wahe Guru Sat Nam Har Haree." Bring your hands in prayer pose on your chest and say, "Har Har Har Har Wahe Guru Sat Nam Har Haree." Really use your navel to chant this chant. You can do this with me on the videos in The Moon She Rocks You program. Repeat this for 3 minutes. The first time you do this, you may not be able to feel anything. With practice, you will feel it really consolidates your energy and reminds you of your identity. The frequency of this exercise works to make your physical body more organized. This grounds and connects your energy in a powerful, positive and joyous way.

When we feel disorganized, we aren't able to do anything. We tend to space out, fantasize, and do lazy things just to get through the day. This kind of lazy day is great when you intentionally want to take a real day OFF. But when that feeling is in control and you need to be in action, take a few minutes to reorganize yourself. You may choose to go to the bathroom where you can be alone, or take a walk out on the street with other people. Chant in a whisper no one but you can hear; chant silently while pumping your navel. You'll be doing yourself a favor, and that's what counts!

The Moon She Rocks You

One night, we were standing in line at a clothing store. The person in front of us was speaking on the phone in Japanese and the one behind us was speaking in Hebrew. It was like the UN and nobody found it strange! So you see, you don't need to worry if you want to chant. Be willing to be weird. No one will care. Remember that being bitchy, depressed, etcetera, is far more removed and weird.

The most important thing is that you're doing what you can to get reorganized, to get back into the essence of you. If you focus, you will find that all of a sudden, you go from feeling powerless and scattered to being cohesive and intact. Feeling uncollected fosters thoughts of worthlessness; you start speaking badly to yourself and end up attracting people who will tell you what's wrong with you instead helping you look at things from a different perspective.

Reorganize yourself. Go get your molecules and thoughts organized so that you can be receptive and projective. Breathing can help you immensely.

Did you know that when you breathe predominantly through your right nostril, you are much more projective and more capable of being the doer? On the other hand, when you breathe through your left nostril, you are more receptive, open and allowing. When you tune into this ability within yourself, you will also be able to recognize it in other people. You will only need to pay attention to what they say because that will tell you if they are projective or receptive.

Being able to intuitively know the situation and organize it so that it can benefit everyone is another organizational skill. This particular gift makes you able to empower others. When in the highly organized Inner Thighs, you can see if someone is organized in their life. But first you learn how you are organized. You must know what pulls you apart and what puts you back together so you know how to thrive in the neutral state. This requires creative strength.

Being creative, means being open to understanding how people think and how their mind is organized. You look at their desks or clothes, and listen to how they speak. You'll know if they are all over the place and not really seeing other people as they are. Knowing this can allow you to see ways to help them feel more organized.

On a personal level, how do you get from the challenged state to the positive or neutral ones where you're really in tune with that creative strength? Well, if you feel your moods are all over the place, just have your hormones checked by a professional. Many times your hormones are at the bottom of it all and the good news is that they can be balanced. It's a wonderful thing how our internal being can get support from the external. If we take certain herbs, we can change the level of hormones in our body and bring them back into a state of balance.

There are so many ways to regulate your moods. We women often say, "It is right before my cycle, so I am entitled to be crazy." Forget it! Who wants to be crazy? It takes up so much energy to be crazy and to apologize to people for being so idiotic. It's useless! Remember, there are people who can help you with this. So go get some help!

We are not on this planet all by ourselves. We are here to have a group connection and it's not just you and the people you live with; it's also your neighborhood and your whole support system. Who are the people in your support system? If you're still building it, make sure you have some really good healers, doctors, teachers, who can help you check the things that concern your body and mind. I offer support sessions, if you want my support, please visit:

http://gurutej.com/private-sessions

If you have a lot of craving for sugar, then your hormones are not in balance, especially if you feel this at certain times of the month. You've heard it before: "I must have chocolate before my period!" or "I need sugar now!" You want those things, but you don't need them. You just feel they will make you feel more connected, less emotional or funky. But if you let the little sugar demon come in to satisfy you, you will turn into a demon. It doesn't serve you or anyone around you and it disorganizes everything.

Take the challenged state in this Moon Center seriously. You would want to use your creativity as you chart this time to say, "Okay, I know the challenge I'm facing and I don't want it to look like it did last month. This time, I will do things that can help me."

When your immune system becomes depressed, you can catch almost anything that comes along and pass the bugs to others around you, your partner, your children, etc. Sickness can steal away so many days of your life. Wouldn't it be wonderful if we could take a day off and do something we really wanted instead of being sick? You have to work on your immune system. There's a lot to learn. My Immune System DVD is the place to start. http://gurutej.com/store/kundalini-yoga-dvds/

Exercise: Bringing Life to the Neutral Aspect of the Inner Thighs

Now here's a really great exercise. You begin by lying on one side and resting your head on your hand. While lying on your left side, making your body as straight as possible, put your right hand on the floor to brace yourself and your left hand under your head. Lift your left leg, chanting Huuuuu as you bring the leg up high as you can, and

156

Laaaa as you bring it back down. Do this for 90 seconds to 3 minutes, then switch sides and repeat.

Keep your inner thighs squeezed towards each other but not touching physically. When you squeeze, you make your inner thighs really strong along with your root lock. When you give strength to them, the neutral aspect of the Inner Thighs, which is driven by creativity, can come to life.

Another fun thing you can do is to lie on your back and put a pillow or block between your thighs and squeeze it. Then do leg lifts with both legs and don't let the pillow drop out. The smaller the pillow or block the more fun and the more beneficial it will be.

Your inner thighs are the border guards of the sexual Moon Centers. But this Center is not about protecting and closing down the genital area. It's also about strengthening it so that you have the power to lift its energy and take it wherever you want. Sexual energy is great if it's timely.

The Moon She Rocks You

If you feel sexually aroused but are alone and need to do other things, pull that energy up and use it wherever you need it. Energy is fluid! The inner thighs give you the power to change the flow of your internal energy. What a gift!

The charting of this Center is very important, and once you get The Moon She Rocks You program, you will have a better understanding of the Inner Thighs through charting. Chart it for three months at the very least and then you will know how good it can be to you. (http://gurutej.com/store/11-moon-centers/)

Creativity, organization, and extra energy—all these will allow you to experience your passion and to discover who you really are in this life, in this time. So squeeze those inner thighs! Love them and realize what you can pull up from them. They can sustain you, they can support you.

Empowered in the Inner Thighs

In the Inner Thighs Center, you have great power in the creative arena, so take on projects that require your creative touch, like decorating, painting, or planting. Cleaning and organization are also great. This energy is valuable. Allow your creativity to rule and it will be a powerful experience.

Disempowered in the Inner Thighs

You may need to clean out drawers, cabinets, closets, desks, garages, etcetera, but you can't make yourself do it. You feel diffused, scattered, and disorganized when disempowered in this Center. You need to consolidate your energy. The exercise that follows can help you out in this regard.

Balancing Exercise for the Inner Thighs

Lasso Pose: This exercise is also known as the energy wrangler.

Duration: 1-2 minutes

Sit up straight. Make fists with your thumbs tucked inside your palms. Have your feet a hip-width apart and squeeze your inner thighs. Move the arms wildly overhead in backward circles. You must move your arms as quickly as possible. Do this standing and make sure the feet are a hip width apart and heels out slightly more than toes. Remember to squeeze your inner thighs. Breathe!

Time is 1-3 minutes. At the end, inhale, hold the breath in and feel the power. Hold it for 30 seconds and then powerfully exhale through your mouth.

The Gift:

Creates clarity and receptiveness; increases the heart rate; very energizing.

Clitoris

Overview

In the Clitoris Moon Center, you are talkative, just like when in the Lips. But the energy of this Center makes you want to socialize and have fun. If you feel really empowered, you will take charge of whatever situation you find yourself in and be the leader. However, if you are unbalanced here, you will be clannish and cliquish, wanting only to be with those you feel safe with or people you are used to, which may not necessarily be the kind of company that is good for you.

The Details

What happens in the Clitoris Moon Center? When we think of the clitoris, we don't exactly think about socializing unless we are thinking of orgies, and we are not. What is this magical little thing called the clitoris? If you have seen The Vagina Monologues, you know that both the vagina and clitoris have more nicknames than you can tell. Still, the great thing that's down there is something that we don't know much about. We are going to talk about both the known and the unknown aspects of this part of our being, the clitoris.

I remember that in the 70s, the big thing was that all women would give themselves vaginal exams. So we all had specula and we'd get down with these little mirrors and we'd look at our vagina. It was amazing to do this because we realized that we don't really .see, much less look at our genitals. Men can see their genitalia; they look at and touch them all the time. We hardly touch ours and it's all hidden, so being able to look at them is very liberating.

Judy Chicago, a feminist artist, created an installation artwork titled The Dinner Party. She created various dinner settings inspired by the genitalia of women: knives, forks, spoons and plates. It was all so beautifully crafted. I remember feeling really amazed the first time I saw it. It was hard to decide which I liked best. I had the opportunity to see it in different parts of the world several times along the years, and each time, it retained its beauty and grace. At the time of its creation, it was sensational and controversial as well as liberating. Today, the exhibit honors women.

162

That's exactly how I want you to feel about this Moon Center.

Where the positive aspect of the Clitoris is concerned, you want to socialize. You feel very outgoing and are willing to connect. If somebody says "social," what comes to mind? Does it mean going to bed with a book? Of course not! You make love, you go out and party, you hang out with your family, you invite the boss to dinner you throw a party, etc.

When the moon is in the Clitoris Center, you want to go out with people or have them over. "I'd really like to go to an opening of something," you might say, or, "I'd love to go to a party with my friends." So, organize a dinner party, have people over for a get-together. This is a great time to do that, to be around people who are important in your life; whether it's for business, family or love because you are going to be very social, feel at ease entertaining them, and making things happen.

You can have your partner invite his or her boss and coworkers for dinner at home. You can also invite a person you want to impress and connect with, particularly anyone who is invaluable to you in business. Make some really great casual meetings happen at this time, and plan a few fabulous social events. Be open to all this happening spontaneously and watch for opportunities that may arise. These will actually help you close all sorts of deals and can heal many types of long time wounds.

The great thing right now is that many people are socially involved in things. Many of us use social networks on the Internet. Others belong to an organization, a club, etc. For example, Paul Hawken, the author of the bestseller Blessed Unrest, created the website www.WiserEarth.com, a directory of more than 100,000 non-profit organizations so that everyone can get connected and see how they can plug in or track what others are doing in their arena. That's simply fabulous! It means more and more people are coming out of their comfort zones, willing to be in the world and to be a part of it. To serve each other in ways we are each passionate about. Find one that is of interest to you and plug into it. You don't have to start your own organization, but you can.

Every big organization is organized as if under an umbrella. Its members all fall under that symbolic umbrella due to their common characteristics. This way, they can be much more powerful and have much more influence. This social leadership which characterizes an organization is also something that you are capable of doing in the Clitoris Center. You can accomplish all of those kinds of things that require vision, foresight, and action. Isn't it inspiring? That's the beauty of this Center. It's where you lead.

What happens in the negative aspect of the Clitoris? Well, you get very cliquish and clannish! You only want to be with a specific group of people—those people you feel safe and secure around, like your best friends. So, if you start to feel withdrawn like that, you will want your people to be in your cave. You know there are other caves out there with other people, but you don't want anybody from those caves invading your cave. In this cave, you want people you already know.

This is not using clannish to help create something but clannish to shield you from the unknown. How do you get out of that feeling?

The Moon She Rocks You

Deep down, you know that you're supposed to be around people that uplift you, who look at you, see your greatness, and push you a little to live up to that greatness. Those are the people who remind you to push outside your comfort zone and into the greatness zone.

Remember, you will always have people who will sit by you in a corner, and that's not bad, but they can also be the shackles that keep you from achieving what you've always wanted to do. Unorthodox ideas that come from you make them uncomfortable. They can't relate to you and are afraid you are going to go off somewhere and leave them alone. Clannishness tries to stifle change.

It may not feel that way, but if you are challenged here, you're not quite where you should be, and you have a nagging feeling there are things you want to do, but are not possible if you stay where you are. The solution lies in connecting with new people so you can step into the neutral state of this Center and think clearly without succumbing to intense emotions.

Clannishness is what I think of as the negative side of the first chakra. Your first chakra is all about your clan, your people, and the place where you were born. Surely, when you were a kid, somebody you trusted told you not to go beyond a certain place because it was dangerous. You believed this, although you had no idea of what could harm you.

If we live our life thinking that it's safer where things are familiar, we will live scared all the time. We will never get to live the essence of life. Life has so much to offer, but you won't receive its blessings if you stay sheltered physically and socially. Get into the game and be part of the cycle of the universe!

Whether we die at day one or one hundred years old, it's important to live the essence of life. Time is not relevant. The positive state of the Clitoris Center gives us the ability to see the need to socialize on a larger scale. The challenging aspect of this Center makes us feel unsafe in the unknown, which is life. We all have days when we feel off, but it's important to get back on track.

Where the Clitoris Center is in the neutral state, you can lead and uplift all the people around you with your charm, your skills, and charisma. You get things done effortlessly for the benefit of all.

Mantra: Staying Neutral and Positive

In order to stay in the neutral and positive states, or regaining those if you are in the challenged aspect, you need to move your whole body freely. Preferably go swimming, running, rollerblading, jogging, power-walking, dancing or play tennis. If you can't, get on the treadmill at the gym. It really does not make any difference what activity or sport you choose to do. Just do something that really moves your whole body and makes you use your core. Otherwise, you are going to sink into this "I need my people" attitude. Even better, participate in a social team sport or take a class with lots of people. You need to do something that takes you out there, clears your head, makes you sweat, and basically changes every part of your being. If you do the activity with a mantra, your body will experience not only the physical, but also the psychic change it needs. I can recommend a lot of mantras to you, but this is the one you really must know. It goes: "Ra, ra, ra, ra, ma, ma, ma, ma, rama, rama, rama, rama, sa ta na ma."

Ra is the sun, Ma is the moon. When you say them together, you get the sun and the moon together. Say, "Rama rama rama rama," then say, "Sa" for birth, "Ta" for life, "Na" for death, and "Ma" for rebirth. Saying this mantra in a quiet whisper is really good, because whispering is the way lovers talk to each other and you need to feel that you are your own lover. By whispering the chant while doing the exercise, you can allow love to come back into you. Do it silently while you are exercising, like when doing the treadmill in the gym. It's super simple and fun! You can get your kids and do this with them in the house. They'll love it! You can march around the house wearing something fun and dance while saying, "Ra ra, ra, ra, mama, ma, ma, rama, rama, rama, rama sa ta na ma." Do it for 3-5 minutes or more, because "more" is better. If you want "yummy" go for more.

Let's talk about something more personal and intimate now. Just close your eyes when you chant the mantra so that it really gets imbued into your being. Play with it; make it your mantra. I want you to understand the clitoris as an extremely sensitive place in our body. Ignoring the clitoris or even removing it, as it is done in some cultures, not only removes the ability to feel pleasure, but also to understand that infinite flow of energy that comes into the body. The clitoris is the most sensitive part of the female body. Many women can only have orgasms from their clitoris. If you like being on top when making love, it's because you get your clitoris stimulated all the time. This organ is the pathway to sensitivity.

In this Center, you should do something that allows you to be sensitive yet grounded so that you can be joyously social, like you're having sex with the whole world. Yogi Bhajan used to tell us, "You have such limited ideas on sex. You only know how to have sex with a partner. Have sex with the universe! Forget about sex as just between two people; make it huge, make it really infinite!" He meant that sex should really be a Divine experience. It has nothing to do with being promiscuous.

Make whatever event you create social, delightful, and so amazing that you get people around you to have a good a time and to achieve that amazing connection that makes everybody walk away ecstatic at the end. So go high, really high! High is the place where everything is vibrated deeply. It's where our grace and our greatness are vibrated at once.

Exercise: Get High on the Clitoris Center

This is a chanting exercise to get you high on the Clitoris Center. Just relax your hands on your lap. If you already have the videos, then you can do this with me. The first thing to do is to close your eyes. You are going to focus on your third eye, which is connected to your clitoris, okay? Chant this all in one breath and repeat that cycle 11 times: Ra Ra Ra Ra Ma Ma Ma Ma Rama Rama Rama Rama Sa Ta Na Ma. Then, inhale, hold, and exhale.

This chant will stimulate you down in the Clitoris but it will also open your third eye. I don't expect you to have this experience the first time, but practice makes perfect. When chanting, be conscious of what happens to your mouth when you say Ra Ra Ra Ra Ma Ma Ma Ma. It's mostly the lips that get stimulated. Different parts of your lips are stimulated by this part of the chant than when you say, Sa Ta Na Ma, when a whole different section of the meridians are stimulated on the roof of your mouth. All of a sudden, you will find out that the glands in your head, the pituitary, thalamus, hypo-thalamus, and pineal glands are open and function properly.

In order to reap all the benefits of this Moon Center, you need to have happy, healthy hormones. Luckily for us, green foods really help the hormonal system. If you think you don't eat enough greens, you can take some wonderful organic powders, like Ormus Greens. I cannot say enough about greens here, but my favorite greens powder is Sunwarrior.

(http://www.sunwarrior.com/affiliate/idevaffiliate.php?id=460)

Greens and exercise keep your whole hormonal system happy and your membranes lubricated. Dryness in the vagina and clitoris often indicates bacterial or yeast infection.

One of the best ways to avoid a yeast infection is to say no to sugar, alcohol, dairy products, wheat, and mushrooms. There are also a few great herbs that you can take in combinations to protect your body from yeast: goldenseal, Pau D'arco, and garlic.

Raw garlic is always better than cooked or dried garlic. Just make sure that everybody around you has a little bit of guacamole. If you don't like guacamole, just put some raw garlic in your salad dressings. Kyolic, or aged garlic extract, is also good and comes in capsules. Hummus. I learnt to make raw hummus and now I'm really good at it, according to my partner. He absolutely loves it! There are all sorts of raw dips and things that you can make that require raw garlic in them. So, use that creative strength to prepare raw dips and stay healthy. Blend things and learn what you can do to keep yourself and those around you healthier—it is magical!

In our present Internet age, social media is the "in" thing to do. The Clitoris is the perfect Moon Center for that! When you are in the Clitoris, you can be the social media queen! You can be out there connecting and have a Facebook party! What's important is to connect and to uplift people making use of your gifts. That's the beauty of this Center.

In the Clitoris, you take the lead. When you are in the positive state, you are in a leadership place, socially speaking. It is a great time to be on a stage, to give lectures, talks, or presentations about things you consider to be very relevant. You need to be out there, to be seen and heard. You also need to be constant and meaningful. For example, when you want to attract followers on Twitter, you post worthy content as often as possible. People start to follow you because they consider you worthy of their time and attention. You're not just pulling them in because you want something from them. You give and share a part of yourself which other people can really appreciate. Being active socially and believing in what you do is all it takes to become a leader. People will naturally and instinctively follow you. Align with the Clitoris Center and advertise to the world that you're someone!

Empowered in the Clitoris

Remember the song from South Pacific "Happy Talkie Talk?" Charming, isn't it? That is you when you are empowered in this Center—you are available, ready to talk and socialize. If you want to feel even better, play with a hula hoop, ride a bike, rollerblade, but most of all, get really present and inside your body and take the lead. Claim your power to lead by getting inside of everyone you are with. It's like having soul sex. Crawl inside them and understand how you can uplift them. This is true leadership. You can have a wonderful time in bed in this Center, and you may want to take the lead.

Disempowered in the Clitoris

You will know disempowerment in this Center if you only want to be with the people you feel safe with. To change this state for the positive or neutral states, you can do special exercises, chants, and meditations.

Balancing Exercises for the Clitoris

Pounding Har: This is the exercise where you clear away anger and cobwebs in your body.

Duration: 2-3 minutes

Sit on your heels on a mat or at your desk if the room is soundproof. Powerfully and rapidly, beat the floor or desk surface with the palm of your hands while saying "Har" (Har means where the finite and infinite merge) with each pounding. Make the sounds come from deep within your diaphragm. This will cause the navel to move with each sound.

The Gift:

This exercise helps to release anger and frustration by using sound and powerful motion to clear mental cobwebs. It also stimulates all the nerve endings in the hands.

Three Part Forward Bend: This exercise is the brain's fountain of youth.

Duration: 1-2 minutes

Stand with legs wide open. The stiffer you feel, the wider you should spread the legs. Bend over and place the fingertips on the floor right under the shoulders or on a pillow or block if you can't reach the floor. Bend the knees if necessary. Inhaling, lift your trunk and head until parallel to the floor. Exhale in three parts—lowering the head and trunk towards your thighs in three equal parts.

The Gift:

The bowing motion activates the spinal fluid up and down the spine and through the brain. It allows your legs and spine to stretch. The resulting enhanced breath helps to release overwhelming feelings.

Membranes of the Vagina

Overview

You are also feeling social in the Membranes of the Vagina, but in a different way. You are social for a cause. You can be in a very neutral space and see beginnings and endings as the same. Things don't faze you. You are extremely calm, cool, and connected. Unbalanced, you feel hopeless as if you were nothing and will say things you would never say at other times, because nothing matters to you.

The Details

The most interesting of all the Moon Centers is the Membranes of the Vagina Center. This is very internally energetic and connective. You long to be connected with something or someone. It can be with only one person or with a million people; the connection itself is the most important to you here.

In the challenged aspect of this Center, you feel like a complete zero. Nada! Zilch! You think your life really sucks, that you are not important, and that you don't belong anywhere at all. Yet you're not even depressed with your situation. Being so numb, unconnected, and unfulfilled, you feel nothing.

When in the neutral of this Center, whatever happens, whatever you think of as good or bad, effective or ineffective, does not affect you at all. It can all come and go and you are just fine with everything. However, that doesn't mean you don't care. Nothing matters and yet, everything does! It's like you're a spectator to a stage where life plays itself out. You want to see what happens next. You understand there is a bigger picture than what you see. You see the unseen; you know the unknown and are friends with them.

The Membranes of the Vagina Moon Center is a really super sensitive place for women. It's a place where we feel intensely. This Center allows you to understand that you will always be connected to a person, place, or thing. It may look like it's either coming or going, but you know that it was a part of you and so will it forever be. That's the way things are in this universe. The nature of the cosmos is that of change and stillness at the same time. It's a paradox. The finite is continuously changing and yet never changing. Through the finite, we can see the changes around us—we age, our old neighborhood grows, the people in the workplace all change—we can see changes everywhere but what most people don't understand is that everything remains the same at the most basic level. The gift of the Membranes of the Vagina is the ultimate neutral mind.

When Yogi Bhajan first told us about the neutral mind, I was about 22 years old. I remember thinking, *Oh, this sounds so boring!* He said matter-of-factly, "You love to ride the roller coaster of emotions, up and down and all around." He was right, of course. We go up and down experiencing the drama and the trauma. We love it until we realize the extent of the pain, and then we go numb. We lose our purpose. It's what usually happens to teenagers wanting to experience the world.

At that age, you may choose to do something reckless because nothing matters to you. This reminds me of the sex slave trade. These young girls are forced to have sex with many complete strangers every 10 to

20 minutes. Numbing! The poor girls have no choice but to go very numb, so that what they must go through does not matter anymore. They feel like a complete zero because they've lost their identity. Even so, there's always hope, they still have a chance to find their true identity. We have a chance to know who we are, with much less challenges than they face, even after we've gone numb. We usually have much less trauma than they experience.

This Center can teach us to understand the infinite pulsation of everything. We get to know ourselves and plumb the depth and the vastness of us. This is the most cosmic of all Centers, and the first lesson it teaches us is to see the difference between having sex and making love. When we make love, we bring our body into accord with the infinite. When we have sex, it just feels good for a minute. Afterwards, we often feel unfulfilled or worse.

The beauty of this Center is that it's a protected area. It doesn't show. It is not on the outside. You can't see it unless you use a speculum and a mirror or look at someone else's Membranes. Knowing how beautiful that area really is and treating it with the grace and the beauty that it deserves, will allow you to experience the inner knowingness of this Center. It has its own radar system. It can let you know who you should partner with in your life and who you should stay away from.

When I first met my partner, I wasn't attracted to the way he looked, but I was attracted to what he stood for, how he lived his life, what he knew, what he experienced, how profound and important that was to him. Now I think he is so yummy-looking. This Moon Center gives you the ability to see the infinity in all and to be extremely neutral about it. If you are choosing a partner with the help of this Center, you are choosing from that vast state of being. If you chose from the challenged zero feeling state, it's going to be disastrous!

Yogi Bhajan always used to say, "You live your life from your five senses, but you should also live it from your sixth sense. Your sixth sense is your intuition and that's the most important sense." Intuition needs sensitivity and this is how it is indelibly connected to the membranes of the vagina. If these membranes weren't sensitive, then we would be numb making love and unable to have orgasms. We wouldn't be able to channel that energy up into our crown and allow it to go out the top of our head or bring it back down. This Center allows you not only to share intimate love with a partner, but also with everything in your life and the universe.

The Membranes are actually little think tanks and they talk to us if we need guidance. We also have a diaphragm in this Center that regulates the flow of energy. The Membranes also allow us to find out what we need in life so this Center can stay juicy, alive, and neutral. What we need to avoid here is numbness.

Recipe: Maca Tea to Heal Hormonal Imbalance

I am a huge believer in Maca, a medicinal root from the Andes known for its energy-imbuing properties. It's used to heal hormonal imbalance and it tastes really good. I prepare it as a tea with a little almond milk in it. Once, it helped me get out of a challenged physical state after eating a greasy vegan version of Eggs Benedict! I was so sick, the Maca made me feel much better. Women are different from one another, and things that are good for one may not be good for another, but Maca seems to be universally really good for everyone. You should at least try it and see what it does for you. You can get this online at www.vitacost.com or a local health food store.

Exercise: Lubricate the Vagina Membranes

As we get older, the membranes of our vagina get thinner and they are much more easily cut and torn. We don't want that. The more work we do to pull up on the vagina and the rectum—called root lock—pulling and releasing and repeating 100 times (remember we used to brush our hair that many times), the more consolidated our energy is and the stronger our vagina membranes get. This is a recipe for a much better sex life.

Another way to keep them really alive and lubricated is to use an alabaster egg. Insert the alabaster egg into your vagina and squeeze on it. You need to squeeze to keep the egg up in there, otherwise it slips out. Don't worry, it will not get lost or stuck inside your vagina. Almond or even good quality olive oil will help if it gets dry during this exercise. You can try this with different-size eggs. Pick one that feels just right inside of you. It works wonders as you grow older. There are also many gels you can use. But do use something because I want you to get your juicy back.

I've heard women in their 50s say the membranes of their vagina are going to become too dry if they don't have a lover and they aren't having sex or so they have been told by their doctors. Don't believe it. I can testify after 17 years of celibacy, that's not true.

How do you stop feeling like a zero or that state where you don't care about things? The best thing is to seek professional help if it persists without cause for longer than a week. But if it is not extreme, try these things: uplift yourself by playing music you love or singing. Put on earphones and sing with the recording. The louder you sing, the better. This will change what's going on inside of your head as the sounds align your frequency and help adjust your hormones.

Music can really help to balance this Center. There is so much great chanting music available online. For example, there are Rootlight.com and Spiritvoyage.com

Exercise: Sipping Breath to Change Demeanor

The sipping breath, done in 4 parts, is one of the best exercises to get out of the numbness you can feel in the challenged state of the Membranes. Take little sips of air through the mouth—four parts on the inhale and four parts on the exhale. Do this for 2-3 minutes. You will find your parasympathetic nervous system going ahhhh. This will really help to change your awareness, coming from a feeling of nothing to a feeling of everything.

Empowered in the Membranes of the Vagina

You are in the mood to socialize. If you can, good! If you can't, that's fine too, since you'd be in the neutral state of mind and heart! There's no blame here, just rejoice in being in the Now—not the small "this minute" now, but the expanded infinite NOW. When you are empowered in the Membranes, you can enjoy almost anything and be grateful for it. This brings out the best in women. Men would love to find us permanently in this state of mind and heart. Enjoy and learn from it while it lasts.

Disempowered in the Membranes of the Vagina

You feel empty and hollow. You can't do anything or have no desire to do anything. How do you release that empty vacant feeling? Go back through the information and exercises I gave you above. Here is another exercise.

Balancing Exercise for the Membranes of the Vagina

Standing Spine Flexes: This exercise serves to give you power, strength, and flexibility.

Duration: 1-3 minutes

Standing with feet parallel to the hips, toes slightly in, bend the knees and place your hands above your knees on your thighs. Flex the spine. Inhale as you arch your back forward, lifting the chin and pushing the chest forward. Exhale as you round up the spine, tucking the chin in. Repeat rhythmically.

The Gift:

Grounding will strengthen the body and head connection and will help to clear the mind.

In Conclusion

Knowledge is power! You are now empowered with the names and positions of the Moon Centers in a woman's body. You know the emotional traits that are expressed in each of them. You know their empowered and disempowered aspects. You have remedies for the challenges. You know that eating right matters a lot and that it is meant to feed your entire being, not just your taste buds.

Grace is your birthright! Power is your gift! Happiness is your cloak! If these keep eluding you, read this book again and plot things out. Better yet, watch The Moon She Rocks You video series or listen to the audios. They will set you on the right path towards a better life. The guidelines will give you grace, happiness, and power.

So, work with those Moon Centers! Meditate, exercise, and listen to your intuition. The results will be priceless! The Moon She Rocks You video series is available to help you. You will get special gifts if you order now.

<u>Moon Centers Bundle Digital Download</u>

- 9 hours of video lessons
- Over 180+ pages of transcripts
- 6-hour audio course

<u>http://gurutej.com/store/11-moon-centers/</u>

Appendix

Exercises

Meditations and Mantras

Recipes

The Moon She Rocks You